AF252157

# HOPE HERE

# HOPE HERE
## Beyond East and West

*by* Norimoto Iino, Ph.D.
Professor of Philosophy
International Christian University

**JAPAN PUBLICATIONS, INC.**
Tokyo & San Francisco

*To International Christian University*
*Its Directors, Professors, Students, and Friends*

Japan Publications, Inc.
Japan Publications Trading Company
1255 Howard St., San Francisco, Calif. 94103, U.S.A.
P.O. Box 5030 Tokyo International, Tokyo 101–31, Japan



ISBN 0–87040–174–2
LCC Card No. 72–81174

First printing: September 1972
Printed in Japan by Kenkyusha Printing Co.

# CONTENTS


Foreword  *vii*

Preface  *xii*

1.  My Hope  *1*

2.  Hope in Hidden Worth  *4*

3.  Hindrance to Hope  *6*

4.  Hope in Haiku  *7*

5.  Hues of Hope  *8*

6.  Hope in Small Things  *9*

7.  Healer in Heaven  *11*

8.  Hope in Hard Work  *15*

9.  Hope in Whole-seeing  *17*

10.  Hope in Hell  *19*

11.  Heterodoxy-honoring  *21*

12.  How to Be Hopeful  *26*

13.  Hope in Humor  *28*

14.  Hopeless  *30*

15.  Hope Hereafter  *33*

16.  The Hope of History: Heaven-defying Dreams  *37*

17.  Hidden Hopes from A to Z  *51*

Letters by Loved Ones  *114*

Under a wisteria tree
  Purple with flowery glee
    I offer a prayer for you

Under the wisteria tree
  A year hence without me
    Think of my prayer for you

Without the wisteria tree
  In all the years to be
    Think of God's trust in you

# FOREWORD

The author of this beautifully written document of a profoundly spiritual interpretation of life is well-known in the
United States both through his teaching in several of its uni-
versities and also through his writings, one of which is *Hints
in Haiku*, published by the Philosophical Library in 1967.

A very considerable part of the beauty of this present book
is its haiku form, which the Author characterizes as the " smallest form of poetry," consisting of only seventeen syllables.
But in this restricted number of syllables, the Author has ex-
pressed commentaries on the principal topics basic to the
major religions of the world. The ideal of Jen, for instance,
which is integral to Confucian ethic, is condensed into the form
of haiku:

> " Jen makes us rise
>     Above fame, gain, blame
>         To be one with the universe "

There is hardly a principal concept in the major religions
which is not illuminated by the Author's insights, formulated
in this style. The Chinese classic, *I Ching*, as well as the Taoist
*Tao Têh Ching*, are interpreted in a way which points out their
rich resources, which offer promise for encouragement to anyone
searching for content and breadth in his life. These ancient
writings, as the Author points out, disclose to us " many universes other than the society of human beings "; and the benefit
of this extended scope of interest is that " our outlook on life "
is thereby enriched and encouraged.

The Author is justified in assuring us that in this document
of his own sensitive life he offers " illumination of hidden

worth " to anyone who sympathetically sees the world thru the help of his haiku and his essays. A moving example of this spiritual excursion, made by means of his poetry and his vast intelligence, is his deeply moving reflection on the cicada which came " into his study " as he was " writing about mercy," and this incident was the occasion for this haiku:

> " The cicada knows
> That I am not interested
> In killing him "

> " So he has come
> To this study of mine
> To end his life peacefully "

A recommendation which is reaffirmed in so many penetrating insights throughout this little book is that " We should try to learn from Nature where cicadas, birds, flowers, clouds streams, rainbows provide us with lessons which should teach us as nothing else could." I think this suggestion will strike a responsive note in the United States, in which so many sensible and sensitive people are struggling to preserve the very riches of which this poet and philosopher speaks. I, therefore, am confident that many who love nature for its inexhaustible treasures for the enrichment of life will be as moved by this book as I have been. I was moved by the gentle imagery with which reference is made to the moon: " The moon says, ' Do not be dismayed, for I am with you always.' " Since I am writing this Foreword on Good Friday, which is so significant in the Christian life, I felt a sort of liberation when I read this assurance about the gentle providence of the moon.

The imagery of nature in this little book is a vehicle of religious and mystical meditation, and in no sense is it a naturalism devoid of an awareness of a cosmic reality, often referred to by the term " God ". The Author is confident that " Peaceful society must be the work of God; but his version of God is as nonsectarian as Cleanthes' *Hymn to Zeus*. The Author makes the striking statement that " Cosmology is the Word of God," and he enriches his concept of God by references to literature as diverse as A. N. Whitehead's cosmology and the cosmology in the *I Ching*. He says:

> " In *Book of Changes*
> Ethic finds its ultimate guide
> In cosmology "

And this is perspective with which this Japanese philosopher and poet interprets Shinto, when he declares in haiku:

> " The Bible of Shinto
> The Beautiful Book
> Of nature with hills, stars, clouds "

The rich imagery with which nature is interpreted constitutes the linguistic vehicle for a theology which is not the impoverished " god language " of contempoary linguistic analysts, but it is as rich in moral insights as Old Testament Prophecy. " God is the Marvelous Mirror which discloses to you your inherent Worth," the Author declares, and he characterizes God as " The Initiator of Incessant Improvement," " The Adventurous Awakener," " Giver of Growth," " Eternal Educator," " Cause of Civilization," and therefore " Our ultimate Hope."

The cosmic role with which the Author interprets God is the same function with which he interprets the Dharma, the reality in whose saving power the Buddhist is confident. The Dharma " harmonizes, pacifies, equalizes." And when he declares that " Peaceful society must be the work of God," he interprets God as he interprets the Dharma. The cosmic function referred to by various terms is the same: " It preserves, sustains, perfects mankind." By virtue of this interpretation, God is " the Lord of human history."

As I read this noble document of faith and courage and hope, I wish that I might have a glimpse of the encouragement which sustains him in his trust that there is an " Initiator of Incessant Improvement," who " helps someone who is humble enough to recognize the work of the Giver of Growth, who ordains all cosmic conditions for the ennobling of human souls." But the fact that this Japanese prophet has this faith is just what accounts for the extraordinary quality of his writing. I could not help but be as moved by his faith when I read the following haiku as when I read the extraordinary expressions of faith of Clement of Alexandria and Origen, who believed that even the Devil would be redeemed by the beauty and goodness of Christ, the Son:

> " There is hope even in hell
> If compassion works there
> Bountifully
>
> The flower of compassion
> Steady, sublime, boundless
> Is hope itself "

Hope is the subject of this moving document of faith of a very great international teacher and philosopher and poet. He characterizes the type of discouraged students with whom he works when he says that " These days I deal with some young students who are not hopeful. They are downcast, cynical, dismayed." If only this blight upon life were confined to the young, it might be accounted for by the fact of youth. But young people are not alone in their " dismay " and their bewilderment. And in this, our common plight, we might find a rich source of help in this book. Its thesis is stated in haiku:

> " Haiku calls our attention
> To hope unnoticed
> In dark nooks of life."

This book generously supports its title, *Hope Here*. It helps us to believe that

> " Hope is what will unite
> All races into one group
> Under God in Us "

After reading this document of faith and hope, I want more than ever before to visit Japan to listen to the lectures of this very great teacher and to see the country in whose long tradition of art, the art of living itself has been so richly cultivated. Every time that I shall read the following haiku, which recalls the early life of this Author, my desire to see Japan will increase:

> "As a child I would
> Accompany my father
> To the Inner Shrine

> Behind it you see
> A pine-clad mount where God Walks
> *Kamijiyama* "

BEN KIMPEL

April 1972
Drew University
Madison, New Jersey

# PREFACE

Illumination of hidden worth in the reader of this book is my aim. As I pen this essay the green bamboo looks attractive. Once it used to sleep in a tiny shoot. There is growth in history. Our dreams come true. God, Adventurous Awakener, views every person in terms of his glorious possibilities of future growth. Amidst the hardest life-situation, He as a Marvelous Mirror discloses to you your future fruition. So believe in yourself beyoud what you now deserve. Your education is a rendezvous with the ideal self of yours. So it is a romance. The cosmic class conducted by Eternal Educator looms large over the horizon.

Appreciation of differences or the ampersand is needed so as to have your outlook on life broadened. Various traditions should learn from one another. This is possible through broad compassion, which is based on the view of the oneness of life everywhere. God is Origin of Organic Oneness.

> Hope is what will remould
> All races into one heart
> Under God's mercy

> Ah world, thou art
> Beating thine own self
> By being exclusive-minded

To President Hachiro Yuasa of ICU, Dr. Ben Kimpel of Drew University, Dr. Hajime Nakamura of Tokyo University, President Takeo Ozawa of Japan Publications, Mr. Norio Okawa, Editor of Japan Publications, Mr. Shigeru Nikki of

ICU, and many other worthy friends I am more profoundly grateful than words can say.

NORIMOTO IINO

April 1972
Tokyo

## *1* MY HOPE

One teacher of English
   I as a child
      Studied under is my hope

His pupils including me
   Would think of him
      As a hope-radiator

He was always kind
   And he was a man
      Of subdued disposition

He is Dr. Edwin T. Iglehart
   Who has inspired us
      So profoundly

His shyness has been
   A source of great encouragement
      To me always

The truly loving glance
   Is one that covers up, veils
      Blesses and heals too

Once a week he would entertain us
   In his home
      So hospitably

His thoughtfulness made us
   Think of God, our Holiest Hope
      In heaven

Almost half a century
  Has passed since then
    And yet he lives in me

His kind words, friendship
  Prayers, songs have sustained
    Me throughout all these years

He has been my hope
  As I deal with students
    From many parts of the world

May he be blessed in heaven
  As he has blessed us
    Grateful friends of his

May he suggest to readers
  Of this book that his humble
    Kind being teaches infinitely

As one grows quiet
  And benign he exerts
    Immeasurable influences

The fact that he is
  An American has been
    Something meaningful

Not a Japanese
  But an American has been
    My first great saint

International friendship alone
  Has taught me
    The true way to good

Indeed the influence
Of a good Samaritan
Has been my hope

# *2* HOPE IN HIDDEN WORTH

In Dr. Iglehart's home there lived a friend of his. Her name was Miss Orpha B. Coe who was a teacher of English too. She was a charming young lady whom many of us appreciated in more than one sense. As to Dr. Iglehart's appeal to me, I should add the realization that he was following God in Christ. Christ inspired many people because he looked at them, not in terms of what they had been in the past, but in terms of their future possibilities. In dealing with ex-criminals, social outcasts, prostitutes he saw through discouraging exteriors into hidden possibilities of moral growth. We parents do that with our own children. But Jesus did it with most unlikely people such as prodigals and the woman of Samaria. He gave them power to become. He continued to love and trust them beyond what they deserved. He saw hope in the hidden worth of their potentialities.

The naive desire of the heart is to be recognized. And there is no moral inspiration comparable in power with that of being unexpectedly trusted and loved consistently, beyond what we actually deserve. Hence Dr. Iglehart's appeal to me. He was a follower of Christ in dealing with his students. He emulated Jesus construed in terms of a unique seer of the hidden greatness on the part of common people in Israel.

These days I deal with some young students who are not hopeful. They are downcast, cynical, dismayed. Hence this book hoping to talk about Dr. Iglehart whose halo is the hopeful insight into hidden worth on the part of men, races, cultures, which Jesus loved and trusted.

> The hopeful man is a halo
> That is the image of Christ
> Hopeful . . .

Christ believes in hidden worth
    In men, races, nations
        God loves hopefully

Iglehart believes in me
    Trusting me always
        Beyond what I deserve

How I would like to inspire
    All the young people
        I am dealing with now

Our hope is the Invisible
    Eternal Insurer
        Of Hope Highest

He reveals the hidden halo
    Of a person who cannot
        Believe in himself

# *3* HINDRANCE TO HOPE

War, poverty, inequality, environmental pollution are problems of this age. These prevent us from being hopeful. Our hope is freedom from these hindrances or disvalues. They are preventing us from realizing our ideals, economic, vocational, bodily, recreational, social, aesthetic, moral, intellectual, religious. Here we would need wide cooperation, interdisciplinary, interracial, international so as to make us well-equipped to solve these problems. Here the centrally important matter is moral, aesthetic, religious. The basic problem to be solved would be the problem of misuse of power.

The religions of the world, Shinto, Buddhism, Christianity would all coincide with the Confucian view of the Harmony of Heaven, Cosmic Challenge to Cruelty, Cosmic Consolation for the weak, Permanent Peace, Perfect Power. The astrophysics of today and modern mathematics cohere with this view of the inspiring order of the universe. Individually and internationally we are urged by this cosmic challenge to be merciful. By removing the above hindrances we are to be hope-kindlers, co-workers with the Heavenly Harmony. The Harmonizer, Healer, Happiness-imparter, Health-radiator in Heaven is Real Reason for religion, Source of science, Cause of civilization. There is Our Hope Ultimate. He is Reconciler of various religions.

Hope has three factors
   Health, happiness, hospitality
     In life here

Health is bodily
   And spiritual
     Enjoying whole-seeing in life

Happiness is brought
   By making others
     Happy, creative, helpful

Hospitality to strangers
   And to God (or *Kami*, *Dharma*, Buddha)
     The Highest and the Best

Hope-kindling is Haiku
   Marking health
     Happiness, hospitality

## 5  HUES OF HOPE

Hope has three dimensions
  Each one of which
    Has a unique coloring

An orientation ahead
  Is able to make one
    Gain stability

An orientation above
  Means insight into
    God, Giver of hope

An orientation eastward
  Counterbalances the trend
    Which is westernization

A ship gains stability
  By a low-placed ballast
    Man gains hope by the above insight

Silvery is the first orientation
  Golden is the second
    Purple is the third

Hope is brought
   Through the habit of mind
      Which sees value in small things

Small things of daily life
   Done well will make
      One blessed and hope-radiating

The summer breeze coming
   Through green willow leaves
      Is uniquely pleasant

Kind words spoken aptly
   Will make the speaker
      Unspeakably fortunate

Helpful hints given to others
   Cause the helpful
      Unexpectedly happy

Japan is a small nation
   But there is hope here
      For dreams come true in due time

Haiku is the smallest form
   Of poetry, in which
      You will see hopeful hints

God is Dearest Dreamer of Dreams
   Which have not been abolished
      But will be fulfilled

Haiku will make you a dreamer
Of dreams like peace, beauty
Compassion, truth, hope

# 7 HEALER IN HEAVEN

As a child I used to accompany
   My father to the Inner Shrine (*Naigu*)
      In the city of Ujiyamada

The Inner Shrine is the center
   Of endearment and reverence
      On the part of Japanese Shintoists

The natural milieu of the Inner Shrine
   Is impressive and inspiring
      To the superlative degree

The crystal clear water of the river
   Near the shrine is so transparent
      That you can see schools of fish in there

There you wash your hands and
   Walk on the quiet path on both sides
      Of which tall cedar trees inspire you

Behind the shrine you see a pine-clad mount
   Called " the mountains where God walks "
      *Kamiji Yama* in Japanese

The Bible of Shinto is nothing but
   The Big, Beautiful Book of the universe
      With its hills, trees, stars, sky, clouds

This Big Book is still and yet speaks
   The inspiring words of comfort, support
      Guidance, encouragement, purification

" Healer in Heaven " is the phrase I have framed
So as to describe something of the impact
Of *Kami* (God) upon my own experience

*Kami* means Above, Superior, Excellent
Purification, Ennoblement, Enlargement
Guidance from Heaven, Healing Mental Wounds

The Bible says something like it as the psalmist
Claims that help comes from the hills
Unto which he will lift up his eyes

The heavens declare the glory of God
And the firmament shows forth
His handiwork from everlasting to everlasting

Jesus takes up this message as he says
God clothes the clover in the field
Causing all things to grow, ripen, flourish

God makes the flowers of the field lovely
Such that Solomon in all his glory was not
Arrayed like one of those beauties

Here Confucius would chime in by calling
Our attention to the harmony of heaven
Which causes the four seasons to recur

The harmonious regularity would be the model
Of benign statesmanship on the part
Of some of the best rulers of the world

Who sees *Kami* (God, Law)? Who misses Him?
Let us mention a few cases
Which are called to my attention now

The prayerful see, the powerful miss
  The merciful see, marauders miss
    The hard-working see, hasty onlookers miss

The humble see, the haughty miss
  The patient see, the proud miss
    The receptive see, the rebellious miss

The appreciative see, the arrogant miss
  The ardent see, the acquisitive miss
    The adventurous see, the aggressive miss

Blessers see, blamers miss
  Coordinators see, corruptors miss
    Dreamers who dare see, destroyers miss

Astronomers see, the apathetic miss
  The admirable see, the antagonistic miss
    Mothers see, ministers miss

The flexible see, the fossilized miss
  The daring see, the dogmatic miss
    The whole-seeing see, fault-finders miss

The profound see, the provincial miss
  The poetic see, the prosaic miss
    The creative see, the careless miss

Hope is in the insight
  Into the ways prestige
    Would corrupt people

Power causes them to be
  Corrupted into " wolves "
    Misusing their prestige

Buddha never succeeded
　His father King of the province
　　Of the Śākya Clan

Christ preferred kneeling before God
　To the kingship
　　In the land of Israel

The natural universe is ordered
　By God, Perfect Power
　　There is hope there

Confucius, Plato, Buddha
　Christ all would see
　　Hope in Cosmic Compassion

Beware of men of prestige
　Worse than tigers
　　Hope is in God ultimately

His will means supporting
　The weak and checking
　　On abuse of prestige

Cosmic Challenge to Cruelty
　Healer in Heaven, or
　　Cosmic Consolation brings hope

God is the only One Lord
　Worthy of our consuming loyalty
　　Our Hope always and forever

# *8* HOPE IN HARD-WORK

Haiku calls our attention
   To hope unnoticed
      In dark nooks of life

People *work hard* habitually
   Here in Japan
      Almost everywhere

There is hope in this habit
   Which bears fruits
      In some unexpected ways

Hope in *humility* which is
   The mother of spiritual growth
      Bringing side results

Hope in *heaven* which is still
   But bespeaks harmony
      Peace, beauty, sublimity

Hope in *home-loving* marking
   Good folk who would build
      A realm of love

Hope in *Hiroshima* which means
   Unreasonable suffering
      Awakening the longing for peace

Suffering accepted and vanquished
   Will add a higher dimension
      To your soul

Japan has borne the cross
Of atomic destruction
To be born into a better land

In Hiroshima God has worked
As Source of Side Splendor
Changing agony into bliss

# 9 HOPE IN WHOLE-SEEING

The rainy day may be tiring
   But tomorrow the sun will shine
      Both the rain and the sunshine count

The past may have been miserable
   But the best is yet to be
      There is hope in whole-seeing

Self-love is natural, deep, universal
   But love of others too can be ours
      So as to make us bigger, higher, nobler

Love of truth, beauty, good, God has been
   The yearning of some men and women in history
      Love of whole-seeing will bring hope

The West is excellent scientifically
   The East is superior aesthetically
      Their mutual enrichment will bring hope

Appreciation of differences will be
   The needed habit of mind in this age
      So as to usher happiness in

Rising above one-sidedness, prejudice, hate
   We can be broad-minded, compassionate
      Whole-seeing in order to stand for hope

The height, breadth, length of life
   Must be all appreciated so as
      To make our whole-seeing hopeful

A synoptic view of life and the world
Coupled with new insights of civilization
Will bring to us hope and bliss

Total Testimony, Autobiography
Of All, Synopsis Sublime
Show God, Hope-radiator Holiest

The Zen master would rather be in hell
     To look after those unlucky folk
          Who are there because of their sins

He can meet them nowhere else
     Hence the necessity of his being there
          In all the years to come until the end of history

This is the spirit of mercy which marks
     The Buddha destined to enlighten all
          In the world everywhere

There is hope in this mercy
     Which would change hell into heaven
          Through the assiduous work of helpfulness

When Japan surrendered in 1945
     The Japanese Emperor and the Empress
          Studied the above story of mercy once again

This mercy in their hearts has enabled
     Japan to be rehabilitated
          Economically, industrially, internationally

There is hope in mercy boundless
     Which can change hell into heaven
          Through fruitful work of helpfulness

Wherever there is hate that is hell
     Selfishness, exclusive-mindedness, arrogance
          Anger, impatience are all signs of hell

Buddha's mercy does its gracious work
   More successfully in hell than anywhere else
      Changing hell into heaven mercy-filled

There is hope even in hell provided
   Mercy works there bountifully
      The flower of mercy is hope itself

Hiroshima was a veritable hell
   On 6 August 1945 when the atom bomb
      Was dropped over that area

But locally, nationally, internationally
   Mercy has done its patient work
      Of making Hiroshima the center of peace
      movements

There is hope in Hiroshima rehabilitated
   Into the unforgettable symbol of repentance
      Resuscitation, wound-healing, peace-making

The whole land of Japan must be
   Regarded as Hiroshima dedicated
      To the cause of mercy, bliss, hope

The whole world must become
   Hiroshima devoted to truth
      Love, bliss, peace, faith, God

# *11*  HETERODOXY-HONORING

In a Buddhist temple in Kyoto City
  I saw chrysanthemum flowers
    Unusually big, graceful, gorgeous

They were the fruit of artificial breeding
  Repeatedly conducted by the best gardener
    For a long period of time

The enhancement of the beauty
  Of the flowers would thus depend
    Upon careful cross-fertilization

Lovelier, more exquisite, more fragrant
  Would be chrysanthemums realized
    Through the art of cross-fertilization

Intermarriage has brought superior children
  Better endowed than their parents
    Physically, mentally, aesthetically

*Taiho*, my Sumo idol, is a son of a Russian officer
  And a Japanese woman, thus enjoying
    Some unique combination of good traits

Long-suffering, hard-working, flexible
  With unusual staying power, having the will
    To improve himself always, has he been

So in thirteen different ways he has been
  A record-breaker in Sumo wrestling
    A handsome man of 187 centimeters and 153 kilograms

Taiho would please Jesus who saw goodness
   In a Samaritan with mixed blood
      Jewish and Babylonian or Assyrian

Heresy-hunting is one of the saddest events
   In the history of religions
      Killing Christ, Bruno, Spinoza

The Judaic-Mohammedan religions
   Have been more guilty of this crime
      Because of their dogmatic faiths

The fossilized finality of old views
   Has caused them to be absolutized
      Thus killing free thinkers, original, creative

Eastern religions like Taoism, Buddhism
   Shinto stand for heterodoxy-honoring
      Ever welcoming new insights of civilization

Lao-tzŭ, the Taoist, would say that true ideas
   Of the Way of the Universe have not been
      Framed in the past as yet

So saying he would appeal to posterity
   To continue to explore new connections
      Hitherto unexplored, unknown, unexamined

A new, exciting vision of a Great Beyond
   Is what Lao-tzŭ would ask us to hit upon
      So as to have us become path-finders

" The best is yet to be," so suggesting he
   Would honor the advance and flight
      Of civilization ever in process

Buddha respected the older tradition
  Of the Vedas without regarding them
    As the final revelation of Truth

The Japanese gardener's dream as he
  Takes care of chrysanthemum flowers
    Would be like that of a star-gazer

Admiring many stars at night
  He would aspire to realize
    What would be more wonderful than them all

" Mine be some figured flame
  That blends and transcends
    Them all," so saying he would pray
      to Determiner of Destiny

A new, pioneering insight or foresight
  Would be a heresy as it is
    Examined from the angle of an old view

Einstein's physics was a heresy
  Before it came to be recognized
    As a more generalized view than Newton's

Since 1966 Yukawa has been expounding
  A new theory of elementary domains
    Which would revolutionize quantum theory

The history of scientific advance means
  The history of the arrival of many heresies
    Gradually to be construed as new orthodoxies

Many branches of modern mathematics
  Are striking illustrations of the arrival
    Of new, fruitful heresies

Buddha learned from the Vedas and yet added
  To them more deeply ethical insights
    While honoring the will to learn from posterity

That is why Buddhism is not left behind
  As civilization moves ahead
    Rather the former gives a creative stimulus to the latter

Buddhism at its most progressive
  Functions fruitfully in every phase
    Of civilization like Japanese culture

Zen Buddhism in particular has taught
  The art of connection-exhausting
    Which has caused science to advance

New meaningful connections have been
  Discovered by Zen-minded Japanese physicists
    And mathematicians like Yukawa, Tomonaga, Oka

Zen has taught athletes like Judo-men
  To realize the importance of what
    " They do elsewhere " before the matches begin

Their food habit, practice of self-control
  The inner poise which enables them
    To sleep well the night before the day of the match

They should gain stamina by practicing
  Regularly for years, staying away
    From liquor, stimulants like smoking, too much meat

Zen symbolized by Buddha's reed-stack
  Means the togetherness of all things
    Including those which Buddha himself did not see

Zen discloses an insight into the togetherness
   Of all things as the reed-stack image suggests
      Urging us to pay special attention to what we have ignored

A theologian who has so far ignored the study
   Of aesthetics or mathematics will be urged
      To begin to understand such a discipline

This new understanding will enable him
   To be a better theologian than ever before
      Because all disciplines are interwoven with one another

# *12* HOW TO BE HOPEFUL

We grow hopeful by having something
  Meaningful to do here and now
    And by doing it as well as possible

A student can do his very best
  In writing an essay, reading a book
    Learning new words, characters, phrases

He should have not only starting power
  But staying power so as to see it through
    Thus he will give a finishing touch to his aim

As in the case of ICU the student
  Will come to know non-Japanese students
    From overseas in order to enjoy international friendship

Thus he will advance the cause
  Of broad understanding, cooperation and peace
    Easing the tensions among the races

He will remove misunderstanding, heal the wounds
  Of the humiliated souls, kindle joy, hope
    And inspiration in some new ways

Academic, athletic, aesthetic equivalents
  Of war he will stand for by being joyfully
    Engaged in university activities

A pretty Japanese girl named Miss Yoshiko Gonda
  Studied at ICU 17 years ago and became
    Acquainted with a Chinese boy named David Lai

David was one of the finest ICU students
  Who have ever studied there, finishing
    The four year course in three years

When she graduated from ICU she became
  A stewardess of the British Air Line
    Flying to London aboard a jet plane

The situation up in the sky is precarious
  And so passengers of the jet would be
    More appreciative of her kindness than on earth

They would have at least some of their race prejudices
  Against the Japanese people examined
    Conscientiously because of her services

So the charming bilingual stewardess
  Served the cause of global cooperation
    High up in the sky, aboard the " meteor "

Later Miss Gonda and Mr. Lai married
  And they have been living in Hong Kong
    As hopeful citizens in that international city

The work of the stewardess may be dangerous
  For her jet may collide with another plane
    But there is hope in the midst of the danger

The bed must be a dangerous place too
  Because more people die there
    Than anywhere else in the world

Danger nobly dealt with opens
  The door to Eternal Enlightenment
    Rooted in Immortality Insurer

# 13  HOPE IN HUMOR

The breeze on a summer day is refreshing
  So is humor in a life situation
    Which used to be barren

Humor is the flower of health, goodwill
  Inner spaciousness, buoyancy
    Will to see the sunny side of life

The will to make others happy
  Is the mother of humor which is
    Different from bitterness, cynicism, taciturnity

Westerners' jokes humiliate the Asiatic
  Unaccustomed to be jovial
    At the expense of his subdued taste

Language barriers aggravate
  The situation where East and West
    Meet, converse, aim to cooperate

I do not come across Westerners
  Whose Japanese is so good as to crack
    Jokes in the Japanese language

" Do not do to others what you
  Would not like to have them do
    To you," this Confucian statement must be stressed

In America social ills like the race problem
  Are temporarily forgotten
    Through the use of wise cracks

But humor at its noblest is
   Derived from healthy motivations
      Which can be hope-radiating

Humor and mercy must go together
   So as to be truly meaningful
      Eventually all values cohere in God, Value Voucher

# 14 HOPELESS

There is hope for all people of all conditions
  Except for those who have unusual prestige
    Like Presidents, Deans, Chairmen

Enjoyment of prestige quickly corrupts
  Those influential people as Plato describes
    Vividly in the *Republic* as *metabolē*

This Greek word means a moral corruption
  On the part of the political head
    Who becomes cruel by becoming influential

No more is he a human being with a heart
  But a ravenous wolf ready to exploit
    All those people with whom he deals

He is not interested in people any more
  But in the increase of power and prestige
    He is enjoying at the expense of others' welfare

If he is well-educated, religious, bright
  He will misuse his education, religion, brightness
    So as to make himself safer, more powerful

So-called Christians have become cruel
  Inflexible, institutionalized, fossilized
    Unable to understand their fellow men

They would humiliate you though they
  Do not mean to do so because they have
    One thing in mind and nothing else

They are interested in keeping their records
   Clean, thus making all the weaker people
      Suffer, weep, grow agonized, be in despair

The haughty misusers of power exclude others
   Thus being excluded from the cosmic circle
      Of Buddha's compassion universe-wide

Mercy is infinitely blessed for it makes
   An infinite number of people blessed
      Thus being rewarded infinitely

Misusers of prestige exclude themselves
   From the cosmos of compassion
      Thus becoming isolated, blind, miserable

Before Buddha was enlightened he had been
   In his father's palace, supposedly enjoying
      Wealth, youth, health but he had never been happy

After he had renounced all the luxury
   Of a prince's life he became happy
      For the first time by making others happy

His teaching of mercy, sharing, above all
   Oneness of all things in the universe
      Made them happy for the first time

And by making true happiness available
   To them Buddha himself became happy
      In the true sense of the term

The notorious murderer Aṅgulimāla tried
   To kill Buddha so as to add to his collection
      Of beautiful fingers but he repented

Buddha would compare Aṅgulimāla
 To a full moon which had been hidden
  Behind the black clouds for a long time

As the moon comes out of the clouds
 Its gleam and lustre would appear
  To be unusually impressive by comparison

Buddha would always be glad to have
 Misusers of prestige repent and switch
  To the way of mercy in which there is hope

When the King of Magadha was killed by his son Ajātaśatru
 Buddha practiced Zen in a most profound sense
  To cause Ajātaśatru to repent

Eternal Buddha must be practicing Zen
 Most enthusiastically to make all cruel folk
  Repent and switch to the way of mercy

Now that the summer of 1971 is ending
 A cicada has come into this study
  Where I am writing about mercy

Perhaps the insect knows that I am
 Not interested in killing a cicada
  He has come here to end his life peacefully

# *15*  HOPE HEREAFTER

The immortality of influence is something
  Which cannot be ignored as we think
    Of the influence of a man like Buddha

He died in 383 B.C. at Kusinārā, India but in Japan today
  He is being thought about with gratitude
    By a majority of the Japanese people

For them Buddha's mercy, words, deed
  Have meant something invaluable
    Uniquely helpful, consoling, ennobling

By following him a human being today
  Will become a Buddha himself
    According to the belief they firmly hold

Not only in Japan but in the rest of the world
  Buddha's merey has come to be appreciated
    Widely, deeply, and with an ever increasing endearment

The uniqueness of this mercy is rooted
  In his view of the togetherness of all things
    Inseparably interwoven with one another

Buddha used the picture of a reed-stack
  Many people must have seen as he was
    Explaining the meaning of mercy

All the reeds are together, indivisibly bound
  So as to make the reed-stack stable
    Thus disclosing the hidden meaning of the world

The testimony of sight discloses separations
  But the insight of Zen inculcates
    The clandestine oneness of all things

Since all things are interwoven with one another
  One's love for another must be as natural
    As one's love for himself, thus uniting self-love with
    altruism

Buddha was merciful toward all men
  Even toward animals, plants, atoms
    Seeing in each of them his only son Rāhula

He saw no enemy anywhere for the so-called foe
  Was part of the whole of which he
    Was part as in the case of a reed-stack

This unusual way of understanding the world would
  Make sense to Buddha himself as he
    First realized it on the morning of 8 December 428 B.C.

But he did not think it wise to preach
  On this insight for those obsessed with
    The testimony of sight showing separations

So he hesitated for some time until at last
  Some superhuman solicitations caused him
    To begin to give the above message to mankind

Oneness of life everywhere is the source
  Of Buddha's boundless mercy whose circle
    Would include all things in all ages

This way of mercy makes a Buddha blessed
  By making others blessed
    Boundless mercy is the only way to blessedness

This is what some physicists like Yukawa
  Would endorse in terms of non-local interactions
    Or elementary domains, material, mathematical, mental,
  space-time

Here the logic is inductive, guided by regularity
  Generalizing itself towards infinity, inclusiveness
    Immateriality marking mind and matter both

Hope Hereafter is the " Ship " of the world sustaining
  The soul now and even after the death
    Of the body, merely a small part of the ship

The ancient Greek scientists like Democritus aimed
  To understand the universe by analyzing
    It into the minutest unit of it called " atom "

The analysis of the atom has grown more and more
  Minute as time passes by until today
    When something amazingly hopeful has been discovered

The concept atom, uncut or indivisible, is now
  Applicable to the whole universe including
    The physicists, and not to its minutest unit

The most precise analysis of matter has
  Opened the way to the vastest whole-seeing
    Enjoyed by the mathematical physicist

This Ship is here but invisible except to those
  Whose eyes of insight have been opened
    Through the practice of boundless mercy

The physicist may see the indivisible oneness
  Of the universe but would be unable
    To connect it with the immortality of his soul

Mercy is an eye-opener, a hope-kindler
    The insurer of immortality to be enjoyed
        By those who live incessant improvement morally

This is reinforced by Paul, changed into a Christ
    As he stresses that nothing, not even death,
        Can separate us from the love of God in Christ

New physics, logic, religion come together
    Thus verfying man's immortality, sustained
        By God, Origin of Organic Oneness, Immortality Insurer

So we have the immortality of influence, inclusiveness
    Interconnected inseparability, incessant improvement
        Infinity, immateriality, induction, importance maximized

# 16  THE HOPE OF HISTORY:
## Heaven-defying Dreams

The hope of history is in you
  If you are a small minority
    Path-finding, creative, adventurous

The majority of people usually
  Are mistaken for they are
    On the side of prejudice, selfishness, greed

Only a small minority can
  Be noble enough to see
    The way out of the predicament

Over 1,000 years before Christ
  The author of *Book of Changes*
    Was a path-finder for China

He stressed the Divine nature
  Of the world in that God would
    Be the Lord of human history

God would give to the noble
  Side results unexpectedly blessed
    Beyond human expectations

The mediocre majority would not see
  The presence of God construed
    As Source of Side Splendor

There the meaning of the noble
  Is explained as the discovery
    Of new, moral improvement for peace-making

Here sex ecstasy is thought of
  As the motive power for peace-making
    When the nations fight one another

As a man loves a charming girl
  So should one nation love another nation
    Generalizing the sex endearment internationally

Such a generalization would be hard
  But be in line with God's will
    Hence the promises of wonderful results

This is a Divine appeal to the minority
  Path-finding, creative, adventurous
    Which you are asked to emulate

Sex love is the strongest instinct
  We have and is to be sublimated
    Into the urge of global peace-making

A Japanese statesman whose wife
  Is American would tend to take
    A fraternal interest in the American people

So this statesman may do something
  Epoch-making in realizing a new relation
    Between the nations he loves

The concept *Judo,* Soft Way, is enshrined
  In *Book of Changes,* which regards
    More feminine ways as the more fruitful

Kindlier, more roundabout, more negative ways
　　Are preferred to more straightforward
　　　　Forceful, spectacular ways of the West

More aesthetically appealing, heart-warming
　　Soul-ennobling ways are better than brutal
　　　　Legal, political, frontal attacks


Confucius would chime in by saying
　　That we should not do to others
　　　　What we would not like to have them do to us

The more subdued way is more fruitful
　　Than the more sanguine way
　　　　Like the positive statement of the Golden Rule

" Do to others what you would like
　　To have them do to you " . . . this may
　　　　Be annoying if you are forcing your taste on others

Your taste may not be what they need
　　Thus imposing on them your idiosyncrasies
　　　　Under the false pretense of good deed

Too much sporadic action and not enough
　　Coordination in line with orientations
　　　　Ahead, above, and eastward

Too much interest in fame, gain, rule
　　And not enough concern about truth
　　　　Peace, bliss, thought, mercy, God

We need creativity which is caused
　　By a wide survey of various data
　　　　Of experiences, hitherto-unrelated-together

A new insight into a Great Beyond
  A charming vision of a new coherence
    Among larger generalizations would be needed

We need mental, academic, aesthetic adventures
  Whereby keener sympathy, deeper understanding
    Higher ideals, longer vistas will be brought

So the hope of history is in a small minority
  Noble enough to be path-finding
    Creative, adventurous and divine

Throughout all the past centuries so far
  The ideal of peace has been merely a dream
    Without being realized in history as yet

The rulers of the nations have been misusers
  Of prestige, whereas the mediocre majority
    Would not dare to be pioneering

The cry of the small minority, path-finding
  Creative, pioneering should be listened to
    So as to realize the dreams of the ages

Dr. Hachiro Yuasa has stood for the cause
  Of international friendship during the past 50 years
    Advancing this cause remarkably

He has his Ph. D. in science from Cornell University
  And Sc. D. from Kyoto University, where he taught
    Later becoming President of Doshisha University

All thoughout the difficult years, 1941–1945
  He stood for Christian internationalism
    And he has been a dynamically creative pioneer

He handled the mililarists even during the heyday
  Of Japanese imperialism with courage and skill
    Representing the minority cause of peace and truth

It was a privilege for me to be his assistant
  Shortly after he was chosen President of ICU
    In 1949 when a group of educators met at Gotemba

Under Dr. Yuasa's leadership ICU was organized
  In April 1952, when 75 able students were
    Accepted into the Language Institute of ICU

President and Mrs. Yuasa have been the hope
  Of ICU and Christendom during the past 20 years
    They have done some adventurous, admirable work

Today President Yuasa is Head of the Board
  Of Trustees of ICU, continuing to guide, inspire
    Sustain us members of the Faculty of ICU

Even the most splendid words we frame
  Could not do justice to the foresight, insight
    Sagacity of President Yuasa at ICU

Throughout all these 22 years Dr. Yuasa has
  Not taken even one day off the heavy
    Administrative work of the unique school

As brilliant as an angel, as steady as the sun
  As gracious as Christ, Dr. Yuasa has been
    Sustaining all members and friends of ICU

He looks youthful, reassuring, encouraging today
  The most high-minded educator this generation
    Has ever produced, he is our hope, guide, friend

May God continue to bless President Yuasa
  In all the years to come as all of us at ICU
    Need his leadership under any circumstances

The ever hopeful guidance Dr. Yuasa gives
  Is based on his unshakable faith in God
    Towering over the wrecks of history

His pacifism, internationalism, trust in all men
  Are flowers of his devotion to God
    The Father of all mankind, Peace Permanent

Dr. Yusa's humility before God has enabled
  Him to appreciate all students whose potential worth
    Is ever looked into despite exteriors

Bigotted militarists may criticize him
  But he draws a cosmic circle of love
    To take them in, thus winning them in the end

His trust in scholars and students
  From overseas is in line with the Christian faith
    In the goodness of the Samaritans

His insight into Zen Buddhism gives him
  Wisdom of Non-discrimination which means
    Profound love for all races, cultures, disciplines

His study of art products, Chinaware, porcelain
  Wall-paintings, Japanese gardens, kimono
    Stone-lanterns has enriched his culture

He is refreshed through his manual labor
  In the way of working as a carpenter
    And taking care of his garden, flowers, bushes

His versatility is amazing, showing
  The inner spaciousness of his soul
    The height, breadth, depth of his being

He has attended more important conferences
  Meetings, discussion sessions than anyone else
    I know, being an expert leader of group activities

His bilinguality is uniquely effective
  In that he out-Americans Americans
    And could out-Japanese Japanese scholars

His genuis is manifested in the reality
  That he grows younger and younger
    More and more sociable, effective, fruitful

Dr. Yuasa is 82 years " young " today, 28 April 1972
  He grows more and more youthful
    More and more hopeful, radiant, original

Rare and excellent is he, for God is
  In him always, making use of him
    As the hope of the history of mankind

He has been living abroad for many years
  And that is why he loves Japan so much
    And that is why he loves all the nations

Intelligent love for one's own country coheres
  With genuine love for all the world
    Patriotism at its best is nothing but love for all

This type of love is the hope of history
  For it is rooted in the love of God
    For all creatures everywhere in the world

> Love gives ungrudgingly, showing a new way
>> Of rising above the tensions between capitalism
>> And communism, between pleasure and pain

At five o'clock on the afternoon of 28 April 1972, the funeral service for Mrs. Yuasa was held at the ICU church. May God sustain and bless Dr. Yuasa and their son, Dr. Yo Yuasa, who will be in Nepal as the healer of diseases and souls. Yo and his wife are graduates of ICU. He has studied medical sciences in England, and will dedicate the rest of his life to the lepers in Nepal. I feel awe-inspired to think about the reasons why he is thinking of this mission. He himself as a boy was not robust. Mrs. Yuasa died on 22 April 1972. So Yo would say, "Be my hope three-parts pain. Let me welcome each sting that bids nor sit nor stand but go." Young as he is, he has faced death more than once. Hence his courage to live creatively.

> The parent of dairy farming in Hokkaido is
>> Mr. Torizo Kurosawa who is the founder
>> Of the Snow-Brand Butter Company

> He is one of the most successful pioneers
>> In the field of education, religion, business
>> Combined into one world of hope

> He too is a youthful genius of 88 years old
>> Having achieved immensely in doing
>>> Things new, original, helpful for Japan

> As a highschool lad he decided to help
>> Mr. Shozo Tanaka who risked his life
>>> By taking a petition to the Emperor for the sake of poor
>>> farmers

> Those farmers in Tochigi Prefecture were
>> Being victimized by the exploitation
>>> Of a copper mine in the mountains

The poisonous elements from the mine
　　Had ruined the ricefields along the river
　　　　But the Diet men had been bribed to keep quiet

Mr. Tanaka went to Tokyo to submit
　　His petition personally to the Emperor Meiji
　　　　As his procession was on its way to Diet Building

Tanaka was imprisoned but gained the support
　　Of genuine people like Mr. Kurosawa
　　　　Who decided to serve the farm in Hokkaido

The dairy farming in Hokkaido is the cause
　　Mr. Kurosawa has been devoted to
　　　　During the past 70 years

His hope has been to change Japan
　　Into the land of milk and honey
　　　　Such as Denmark in northern Europe

Love for God, all men, and soil is the ethic
　　Which Mr. Kurosawa has seen in Denmark
　　　　And this love he has been upholding

He has been stressing the idea that Japan
　　Like Denmark should see in the national ruin
　　　　The chance to gain industrially what she had lost in the
　　war

So he would urge all people in Hokkaido
　　To begin to raise cows, work hard in the spirit
　　　　Of loving God, all men, and soil

Mr. Kurosawa has organized the Dairy Farming University
　　And two other schools near Sapporo, Hokkaido
　　　　So as to teach the art of dairy farming

All these enterprises of his have been
   Amazingly successful chiefly because
      Of his love for the workers helping him

He is the finest Christian businessman
   Pioneering enough to share his gains
      With all of them, gratefully working with him

His foresight, generosity, fairness have breathed
   Into his work the breath of inspiration such
      That all the workers cooperating with him are one in
      spirit

Too many people flock to big cities
   Like Tokyo these days and so Mr. Kurosawa
      Would teach them to come to love the farm

The farm is where health, hard work
   Religiosity, noble ethic, patience, ingenuity
      Cooperation, beauty, stillness would mark the people

The introduction of dairy farming would
   Improve on the diet, the physique of the people
      And their standard of living

The cattle would make the soil rich
   Because the manure, urine, and other things
      The animals give to the soil are fertilizers

Mr. Kurosawa would prove the existence of God
   By saying that new pioneering, creative views
      Of man and society have been revealed
         To mankind from time to time

Denmark over 100 years ago was ruined
   By the war which had taken place
      In Europe but she has been rehabilitated
         Into a new, vigorous, healthy land

Men individually may be corrupted
  But they will be regenerated into new men
    Of moral integrity, high ideals, and hope
      Through the Unseen God who is at work

The creative genius of Christ, Plato, Buddha is
  Heaven-defying, dreaming the dreams
    Of just society modelled after Heaven

Exciting, breath-taking, unique
  Is this genius, filling mankind
    With some awe-inspiring gratitude

The medieval period in East and West
  Is imitative, stale, domesticated
    Without the cosmic flare of originality

Conservative, second-hand, following
  The pristine, path-finding, epoch-making
    Challenge of the antiquity

Panic of error is the death of progress
  The medieval mind is safe, tame, stale
    Without rising above the ordinary

The glory of the new age of ours would be
  The hope of the spirit like that
    Of the mathematician Galois assassinated, aspiring

The parent of a better future will be
  The adventure to dream, dare, do
    Deviate from the path of fixity, boredom, death

The adventure of height, breadth, foresight
  Unique in content, coloring, combination
    Aiming to fulfil the highest hope

Sublimation of sex, science, statesmanship
   Into merciful use of power is what philosophy
      Would have to realize under God's guidance


Order is hard to realize in human society
   The cosmic order is maintained by God
      Overall Orderer, Origin of Organic Oneness, Permanent
         Peace


Merciful Mathematician, urging us to see
   The mathematical structure of reality
      In terms of conjugation symmetries infinite-dimensional


God is Marvelous Mirror disclosing to us
   Our inherent worth so as to change us
      Into citizens of healthier society
         Where they become hope-kindlers


Source of Self-confidence on the part
   Of frustrated people is God
      Because of whose gracious guidance
         There is hope in the imprisoned splendor


      Under a wisteria tree
         Purple with flowery glee
            I offer a prayer for you


      Under the wisteria tree
         A year hence without me
            Think of my prayer for you


      Without the wisteria tree
         In all the years to be
            Think of God's trust in you

The Cosmic Jubilee
  Ever splendid to me
    Bespeaks God's love for you

Fame and money cannot bring bliss
  This is the religious claim
    Verified in this age

Perhaps Yasunari Kawabata had
  A sense of responsibility too great
    To be fulfilled by any one man

On 16 April 1972 our Nobel Prize
  Novelist killed himself
    For some mysterious reason

Like many distinguished novelists
  Of Japan he died
    At the top of his brilliant career

The average man finds it
  Difficult to understand
    Why men of genius commit suicide

Perhaps Kawabata had needed
  A good rest so as to ease
    The tensions in his mind

Despite everything we should
  Continue to do our work well
    Under the grace of God

God is Shame Sublimator
  Urging us to rise above
    Whatever burdens we bear

The Cosmic Cross-Bearer
    Helps us carry our crosses
        With courage and hope

The Hope-Kindler Par Excellence
    Lives, wisely conducting
        The Cosmic Class, answering our prayers

So much work must be done
    By all of us always
        We must live on

Let us be hope-radiators
    In some dark nooks of society
        Where suicide is thought of

Health-restorers, cancer-curers
    Suicide-stoppers, hope-imparters
        We would like to be

The West is man-centered. The so-called wisest of Western men, Socrates, would say to a fellow-citizen of his, "Know Thyself." This tradition coupled with the idea of being led by sense-perception like the testimony of sight, would bring those who are self-centered. The past is gone; the future is not here; what the naked eye cannot see is labelled "gone." God is dead. The high ideals like self-enlargement, self-ennoblement, self-transcendence, justice, equality, mercy cannot be seen with the naked eye. Only the tall, impressive-looking, white-complexioned, blonde Caucasian people are visible, real, important. Hence Hitler's slogan: "The Caucasian master race should rule the world." The implication of this utterrance is that Asiatics are inferior, should be serving the White master race, must not come onto the same high level of civilized life. More than once in history China has been victimized as the above view was put into practice, by Westerners, including soldiers, statesmen, travellers, missionaries, philosophers.

Chinese classics like *Book of Songs, Shih Ching,* 詩経; *Book of Changes, I Ching,* 易経; Lao-tzŭ's *Discourse on Morals, Tao Têh Ching,* 道徳経 are suggestive in disclosing many universes other than the society of human beings so as to broaden our outlook on life. According to Chuang-tzŭ's *Free Play of Mind,* a sage may take a nap in which he dreams about a butterfly visiting many lovely flowers. But as he awakes he is a Chinese thinker again. Here he does more than what the French philosopher Descartes does by doubting as to whether he is a human being or a butterfly. Maybe he is a real butterfly thinking about a Chinese sage. This is Chuang Chou's 莊周 thought which humbles us to realize that we may be butterflies after all, unable to realize God, mercy, peace, hope, righteous use of power. We cannot fly like butterflies either. We are unable to appreciate the beauty of flowers. We fight, ruin kingdoms, cities, civilizations. The butterflies are not so destructive as men and nations are. They are not responsible for environmental pollution of this age of ours.

Chuang-tzŭ's story of the Big Bird, Taiho, is the fruitful realization of a dream. As the big fish becomes the Big Bird, flying from one corner of the sky to the other, a tiny cicada would wonder about the necessity of such a gigantic flight enjoyed by Taiho. Today America and the Soviet Union are able to make their astronauts fly to another planet, a tiny cicade on earth wonders about the real purpose of such an expensive flight, scrutinized from the point of view of making human society better, nobler, more peaceful. Men seem to be better educated than cicadas in some respects. But are we morally better than the cicadas? We are misusing the knowledge and power we have. We make history so noisy, demoralizing, unstable. The cicadas make music. But the noises made by human cities are horrible. The cicadas do not seem to be so sexy as some of us. We should try to learn from Nature where cicadas, birds, flowers, clouds provide us with lessons which should teach us as nothing else could. The classic literatures of the Chinese antiquity stress that True Teacher, Eternal Educator, Peace-Amity Engenderer is at work in Nature. The cosmic class is the only successful school of learning, whereas no human educators should be so presumptuous as to monopolize the task of education. Upon the contrary, all human educators are invariably unworthy to be deserving the high mission of teaching the students. Thus a most basic self-examination would be required of human educators, statesmen, all public servants. Especially philosophers must learn from the Chinese antiquity whose wisdom is refreshing to those who are obsessed with human society alone. This obsession will ruin the future of mankind.

*Book of Songs* (c. 3,000 B.C.) is a collection of folk songs. It mentions bamboos growing harmoniously in the grove, show-ing a beautiful cooperation, coordination, unity among them. This could teach men, races, classes, nations lessons of harmo-nious living. Bamboos never ruin one another. On the other hand, the Emperor's palace is a theatre of misuse of power in that good, upright men are put to shame, while cruel men who know how to polish the apple with the influential courtiers are enjoying the positions of prestige.

The Chinese antiquity has its Bible in the Big, Beautiful Book of the universe. No primitive book full of ideas incoherent with one another would be dogmatized, fossilized, absolutized. As in the case of Mohammedanism such a primitive revelation-claim would be inconsistent with new findings of science, math, philosophy, thus killing many free-thinkers interested in reinter-preting the meaning of their book. The history of the West is full of victims caused by dogmatic upholders of their Bible which has prevented mathematical science from advancing. Bruno, Spinoza, Gauss, Galois, Russell are only a few of those heroic souls whose creative originality and love of coherence has put them in difficult positions. So in the West, the tap root of prejudice and persecution has been seen in the theological attempts to absolutize the primitive tenets of religion, enshrined in the Bible or Koran. This is in line with the claim made by Gordon Allport of Harvard University. Cf. his *Nature of Pre-judice*.

The Law (Dharma) or Disposition of the Universe is God. He harmonizes, pacifies, equalizes. He is Explanation for Every-thing orderly in the natural milieu. This makes a marked contrast to human society where disorder prevails in all history. Order is no accident. Wherever there is orderliness as in the case of Nature God is at work as Overall Orderer. This Divine Order is infinite-dimensional. Beauty, harmony, mean, Yin-Yang conjugation symmetries, mathematical patterns of all kinds are suggested in *Book of Changes* and *Book of Songs*. Change, growth, group, advance are some other ideas enshrined there. These mathematical ideas were ahead of the age in the Chinese antiquity. These would give mathematicians creative stimulations. It takes modern mathematics to begin to fathom the depth of each of the above ideas found in *Book of Changes* which definitely proclaims, " Mastering mathematics, prophesy the future happenings." This would please Dr. Nobert Wiener of Massachusetts Institute of Technology for he did some creative work in writing *Cybernetics*, which is intended to be the scientific ladder for guiding mankind in the direction of globlal cooperation and peace.

The idea of the middle or mean marks not only *Book of Changes* but also Buddha, Confucius, Plato, Jesus. The Yin-Yang harmony, the soft-hard mediation, God's intermediary task mark *I Ching*. Buddha would avoid the two extremes of luxury and self-torture, thus hitting upon the middle way to self-realization. Confucius would construe the idea of the mean in moral terms so as to teach men neither to do too much nor to do too little. Jesus is Mediator between God and mankind. Plato would construe it mathematically, $(1+3)/2=2$. Here the number two is the mean between one and three. Modern math would construe the mean in more generalized terms in connection with mean value theorems in differentiation and integration. Probability theory is rooted in the Central Limit Theorem, which is one of the most wonderful ideas of math today. The idea " Central " is rooted in *Book of Changes* which mentions God as " *Limit* " *Luminous* 太極 causing the Yin-Yang to come closer and closer to each other till both become one harmonized unity. The concept " Theorem " is derived from Plato whose contemplation (theoria) of all time and all existence alone would disclose the true meaning of any idea, whether it be matter, mind, God, *The Republic*, 486A. The Central Limit Theorem means something of the assurance as to the disclosure of the math pattern called the Gauss Error Function, if and only if a large number of cases, whatever they may be, are taken into account.

Quantum Theory is a set of statistical averages. Averages are means. The uncertainty principle and other considerations would necessitate the physicist to be guided by statistical averages and not by one-to-one correspondences between theories and observables. The average value is the only thing having physical significance.

Lao-tzŭ's *Discourse on Morals* makes it clear that the past definitions of the Way of the Universe are all inadequate. Better definitions of it would have to be framed in the future years. This warns against the possibility of our freezing the revelation claims of the grey past. Be dynamically original, creative, path-finding in your search for truth. The best is yet to be. Be forward-looking. This teaching Lao-tzŭ gives has been best exemplified by modern mathematicians like Georg Cantor who counted infinity, thus initiating Set Theory, or A. Galois who revolutionized mathematics by introducing Group Theory based on the ideas of identity elements, inverses, functions. New physics of this century also comes under the category of original adventure, which Lao-tzŭ would endorse.

Common sense must change its stereotypes like this: The West is forward-looking and China is backward. The Chinese antiquity has been ahead of the age in stressing the need of the cosmic flare of originality. The religions of the West are backward-looking, fossilizing primitive dogmas of the most dangerous kinds. The wrath of God modelled after a tyrant is a case in point.

*Book of Changes* would view the sage embedded in the harmony of heaven. Equality, harmony, order, regularity, beauty, peace, sublimity of heaven are emulated by him. Hence his moral integrity. Such a sage is the ideal ruler able to realize fairness, merciful use of power, peace, happiness in human society. The great man 大人 shows the disposition of heaven and earth, the orderliness of the four seasons, the law of the universe. His disposition is Jen which Confucius makes famous by construing it as the most compassionate use of the prestige of statesmanship at its noblest. It is the opposite of tyrannical abuse of political influence. Whenever people do good work he would give them credit for that. Whenever there is difficulty anywhere in society he feels responsible for that. He knows how to save the face of the loser. He would not humiliate the defeated. He is the living example of the order of heaven down in human society.

The order of heaven will be increasingly disclosed to men through aesthetic, academic, athletic activities on the part of scholars, scientists, statesmen. Music at its noblest is a human means whereby heavenly order is revealed to men. Painting at its best would be another way of emulating the beauty of Nature. Like a landscape painting, the finishing touch given to it would be a thin coating of white power put all over the canvas, as in the case of a girl's facial makeup, with painted lips, cheeks, forehead with the final finishing touch given to the whole make-up by a thin coating of white power perfumed. This finishing touch is Li, decorum, propriety, 礼 which makes a difference to statesmanship at its best. Not just economic values but aesthetic, academic, athletic values would count here. The ruler must study continuously so as to know the order of Nature. Athletic activities like archery would nurture the moral character of the ruler, as well as his physiological constitution. Man is more than a body. But the body must be in the best condition so as to function as a noble part of Nature in whose order the man's spirit must be embedded coherently.

Even a cynical genius like Bertrand Russell would praise the wisdom of China, by pointing out the way China would see things in perspective. Russell had been expelled from his Alma Mater, Cambridge University, where he had taught philosophy but insisted on pacifism at the outbreak of the First World War. He went to Russia, finding nothing truly enlightening there. From there he went to China where he would see among Chinese intellectuals Spinoza's dream of viewing things in perspective realized concretely. Chinese sages have poise, perspective, profundity. This Russell praises.

The Confucian ideal of Jen is spiritual, while the Western democracy is legal. The former is conscientious, ethical, aesthetic. The latter is forceful, external, cruel. Jen is centrifugal in the sense of the ruler's taking the initiative to examine his inner life in line with the order of heavenly harmony, then moving to the next concentric circle (home), then to the office, the government of his own, finally to the outer-most circle of the world community to be regulated in line with the same principle of the order of Nature. This is Jen. The Western idea of democracy would be centripetal in that the world or people outside would try to check on the misuse of power on the part of the ruler in the center of the circle.

The mutual enrichment of East and West here would mean the conjugation symmetry of Jen and democracy. When an S. Radhakrishnan of India functions as President he would be able to realize this mutual enrichment politically. This was the ideal of Martin Luther King, Jr., who like Abraham Lincoln was assassinated by the ignorant idiots.

Chinese ideals are international, interracial, global. In this atom age of ours we are appreciative of these wide interests. One world or none. Eventually all the nations or races either rise or sink together. This is the inevitable requirement of the new age of ours. The Zen claim of the oneness of things is being verified by the international happenings of this age. Also the Zen view of togetherness of the three generations, past, present, future must be taken seriously. *Book of Changes* continues perpetually to teach mankind in this age: Master mathematics and prophesy the future events. We should not function sporadically but have an orientation ahead so as to give us stability now. So to the West we of the East would say: "An orientation ahead, an orientation Eastward, an orientation above would be needed." The best Chinaman is the best citizen of the world. The best citizen of the world must be the best citizen of the universe in which True Teacher, Eternal Educator, Insurer of Immortality has been functioning all the time. As men emulate the cosmic order, becoming one with this order, they will be immortal as part of the whole cosmos, thus giving us the assurance that Insurer of Immortality gives us Hope Hereafter.

Here the reasoning is not so atomistic as a Western proof for immortality. It is whole-seeing, coherent with the testimony of physics which today sees an inseparable, indivisible universe at the quantum level of precision. The concept atom (uncut) now means the whole universe which is uncut, inseparable, indivisible. This is the modern verification of the philosophy of Zen once hit upon by Buddha at the foot of the Bodhi Tree in 328 B.C.

## A. Both And

Fancy ideas dart across the imaginative mind. The mating of East and West is hinted at by the Yin-Yang myth of *I Ching*. The masculinity of the West is shown by the Aryan Invasion of India or the American Intervention in Vietnam. India, China, Asia in general would be more feminine. Enduring the pangs of shame, shock, slander, the East has been showing its grace. Christ Conquering is a Western product, while Christ Coordinating would be the Eastern faith. Lao-tzŭ, older contemporary of Confucius, 552–497 B.C., would honor non-action. Human action is rude. God is Sublime Stillness. This would please the French mathematician Galois, 1811–1832. His group theory is made possible by identity elements whose operation on other elements would not make any difference to them. So non-action on the part of the identity element sustains all the functionings of this theory. In other words, non-action is God. This line of reasoning would make the Eastern view of Christ more subdued than the Western view. The East would identify pacifism with the cause of God in Christ. God is Peace Permanent, Infinite Identity Element, Notable Non-Action, Supreme Subdual. When we do not know what to do we should be still. When we realize that we are doing something bad we should repent. Individually and collectively men have been repeatedly making mistakes. Misuse of power has been causing too many victims everywhere in history. Too often the nations have fought, thus ruining innocent non-combatants. Especially in this age of ours, the use of absolute weapons over cities like Hiroshima, followed by nuclear testings repeatedly conducted would be sinning against the cause of mercy. Not action but non-action would be more nearly right. Prayer means for a Christian to be doing nothing but be alone in a quiet place so as to listen to God. Zen means for a Buddhist to be alone in the bosom of Nature so as to concentrate on the meaning of cosmic coordination which is able to sublimate him into a compassionate self. Here is non-action meaningfully exemplified. The right orientation must come before action is taken. Here too is the meaning of non-action whose value is often minimized. Non-action is the necessary basis for concentration, deep thought, self-examination. The West has been stressing action naively, without realizing the interdependence between good deed and non-action.

The Western civilization can be traced back to the concept of the atom, uncut, $\check{\alpha}\tau o\mu o\varsigma$. The atom means the ultimate unit of the universe materially construed. It is the individual of the Western civilization. The Chinese individual is the invisible harmony or peace of Nature. This harmony is not sense-perceptual. It is aesthetic, intuitive, cosmic. *Book of Songs* and *Book of Changes* would stress this harmony as the disposition of Reality, God of Peace, Yin-Yang Harmonizer. Here we see the origin of the more spiritual view of the universe. The mating of East and West would mean the union of the spiritual and material views of the universe. The spiritual view would teach peace, coordination, harmony, coalescence construed as the will of God. The West would stress the need of material, economic values, hard work in acquiring necessities of life, pragmatism, business administration, industrialization. Here my hope is a wise harmonization of the Greek and Chinese interests. Appreciation of the " ampersand " which means the symbol &, " both and." Today Japan is more interested in the Greek interest, slighting the Chinese concern. This is due to westernization pursued at the expense of the above mating. Atomic energy has been released by elementary particle physics whose sad by-product is the Hiroshima catastrophe in 1945. It is the irony of history that Japan has since been interested in the acquisitive bent just the same, without giving more thought to a happy mating of the two concerns, Chinese and Western.

In the 13th century B.C. the Aryan race in the Caucasus area invaded India, thus conquering the aborigines of India in a short period of time. But the Aryan victors became conscientious so as to come to regard the vanquished as dear members of society. This stress on hospitality to the estranged is enshrined in the sacred scriptures of the Vedas which are the most ancient Bible of the Indian people. The Vedas would have commentaries attached onto themselves. The Upanishadic writings are those commentaries which check on the Vedas from the point of view of coherence among all the data available to the Upanishadic philosophers, who mention the Atman-Brahman union as the highest of their religious experience. Atman is derived from the idea of breathing or aspiring ($\dot{\alpha}\tau\mu\acute{o}\varsigma$, $\ddot{\alpha}\omega$, breathing), thus explaining the religious meaning of the self praying to be like the Absolute, Vastest, Brahman, God. So the Indian view of the universe is spiritual, religious, moral in that the minutest unit of the universe is spiritual, not entirely different from the Supreme Spirit, God. This Indian cosmology reminds me of the new view of our century in that at the quantum level the universe is inseparable, indivisible unity, including the physicist observing it. Matter at this level is fluid, not entirely different from the mind. Both are energetic activities whose mediator is mathematical such that the British scientist Sir James Jeans would see in the universe the Great Thought of a Pure Mathematician, God. The Nobel Prize physicist C. N. Yang would regard Nature as the realization of mathematical ideas like Yin-Yang conjugation symmetries. Dr. Hideki Yukawa's new ideas of elementary domains are the ingenious union of elementary particles and the Indian view of the smallest unit of time, kṣaṇa, 刹那. This unit of time is seen in the Buddhist philosophy of Dignāga, about 400–480. He would see the truly meaningful concept of "individual," svalakṣaṇa, in the present moment (kṣaṇa). The philosophical meaning of time construed as the stuff of which all events are made cannot be ignored, neither by philosophy nor by natural science. Yukawa is a philosophical physicist who sees the necessity of explaining matter in its context of space-time in line with Einstein's general theory of relativity. So Yukawa's new view is like the cosmology of the mathematician-philosopher, A. N. Whitehead who explained all things in terms of a set of occasions united into the whole universe by God, Principle of "Concretion," making all of them "grow together."

Here the mating of India and Greece means the contemporary unification of feminine time (kṣaṇa) and masculine matter (atom) such as to frame the new view of the indivisible, inseparable, uncut oneness of the universe. This is another example of the new verification of the Yin-Yang marriage prophesied in *Book of Changes*.

*Book of Songs* is a collection of poems composed by Chinese people way back in history. Appreciation of the Ampersand here means that of poetry and philosophy. Heartfelt poems which stand for the true experiences of the masses of people are often more deeply philosophical than dull class-room lectures given by professional philosophers who are out of touch with the hopes, fears, dreams of the general public. *Book of Songs* is moving, inspiring, hope-kindling, joy-spreading. Today philosophy lectures in a university might be boring or put the students to sleep. They may be too hard to understand, too untrue in relation to life situations, too devoid of the thrill, poise, romance of the adventure of the world. The sailing clouds, rainbows, hues of the hill, the music of the forest, butterflies, cicadas, flowers, lakes, rivers bespeak a wonderful tale of the task of the peace-loving God. All these sights, scents, sounds of Nature plead for the need of harmony, peace, happiness on the part of men who are urged to emulate the panorama of the natural events. Philosophy must be akin to poetry. Poetry at its best is philosophically meaningful. The mating of the two is a necessity. Both are gifts of God.

*Book of Songs* appeals to the reader because of its vivid representation of the music of Nature. This music is too rich in meaningful hints to be put into human music, however noble it may be. This cosmic music is the source of all civilization with its art, aesthetics, ethics, politics, philosophy, mathematics. The best ruler must be a good musician, who prays for heavenly harmony to be breathed into the administration of the government. Thus and thus alone can society be growing peaceful. Then the people will begin to be well-fed, well-sheltered, well-contented. Misuse of power would have to be sublimated into merciful use of it through this vision of heavenly harmony. This appreciation of cosmic music goes with the appreciation of mathematics stressed in *Book of Changes*: Master mathematics so as to make prophecy fruitful 極數知來之謂占. The mating of music and mathematics is a Chinese hint whose creative possibilities have not been appreciated fully as yet. Math at its best is free, beautiful, infinite-dimensional. It is the most creatively free activity of the human mind in that the initial axiom of the older math like Euclidean geometry has been freely, basically, frankly re-examined by modern mathematicians so as to frame new geometries. The universe of math may be likened to a cosmic chrysanthemum with an infinite number of exquisite, fragrant petals. It is beautiful but not boring because unlike a flower it does not wither away but grows more and more multi-dimensional as time passes. Its multi-faceted richness and its unity are wonderful. These days modern math abhors the brute force case-by-case exhaustion method, preferring the light, deft, delicate touch of the zero-infinity perspective. It does not so much count as accounts for all possibilities in some highly complex situations. Since every science, natural or social, grows more and more mathematical as it advances, the whole course of civilization becomes more and more mathematical. Nations like the Soviet Union do not honor Zen, Jen, Tao but respect math whole-heartedly. Hence the meaning of math serving as a mediator between Communist nations and Buddhist nations.

The "soft way" or Judo 柔道 is a well-known phrase in Japan today. This Japanese art of self-defense must be traced back to *The Book of Changes* where the phrase appears. There it means the Yin (feminine) tactfulness which brings the fruit of the middle way 中道, which means moral supremacy. Not hardness but softness 柔 would be in line with the way of God. Softness means obedience or loyalty to God. The four seasons obey the will of God, thus enjoying regularity, order, harmony. The sage is so flexible as to be one with His will. Hardness would mean disobedience to God's way. This is the reason for the disorder of human society. Peaceful society must be the work of God, to whom it is obedient. The soft way leads men to God who maintains order, peace, bliss in Nature. It preserves, sustains, perfects mankind. Here is the disclosure of the hidden meaning of Non-action to which Lao-tzŭ would call our attention. When men obey the will of God, through this non-action on the part of men, human misuse of power ceases. This brings order, peace, happiness in history. When Heaven is the ideal of human society the latter will begin to take on the order of Heaven. As a psalmist would say, "Be still and know that I am God". Human misusers of power like Herod, Napoleon, Hitler would have needed the message of non-action and the soft way.

In this connection Mo-tzŭ, c. 479–c. 381 should be introduced. He was born in Lu, which had produced Confucius. Being a son of a poor despised family belonging to the lower class, Mo-tzŭ was tattooed, thus being set aside as an ex-criminal. He would stress three ideals such as universal love, unconditional peace, seeing political wisdom in members of the despised class. Influential people of the higher classes are all morally corrupt, aesthetically blind to the sufferings of the poor people belonging to the despised class. As to the above ideals of love, peace, wisdom, they are symbols of the will of Supreme God 至上神.

Mo-tzŭ's view would mean something like this in a contemporary situation. In the U.S.A. a member of the black people, say Martin Luther King, Jr., should be the President. Then the Vietnam War will stop. The black people will be more respected in U.S.A. Other minority peoples in America will be able to say more about the policy of the U. S. Government. Love for the despised classes will replace the shameful way they are dealt with. So eventually the White Americans will be happier, enjoying the peace of the world. The ways the White Race continues to be politically dominant in America is suicidal.

Mo-tzŭ advocated a mild form of social revolution. He would not change everything in the status quo, but retain whatever is in line with the will of Supreme God. Whatever in society that serves to further the causes of peace, love, wisdom must be preserved. Whatever is against them must be changed. And the angle from which to view society must be the angle of the Divine orientation, whose colors are love, peace, wisdom. Mo-tzŭ was interested in Law whose authority would have to give as much weight to ethics, statesmanship, religion. Thus he would regard religion as inadequate in making a difference to social improvement unless it is reinforced by Law, ethics, statesmanship.

Some Chinese scholars deny that Mo-tzŭ was tattooed and an ex-criminal. But it seems to be true that he put himself on the side of despised people down at the bottom of the social ladder. In sympathy at least, he was one of them, representing their fears, longings, prayers. He would be engaged in manual labor, making parts of the wheel to be used for a cart. All this would make a difference to his political view. Self-transcendence is difficult to realize, however morally desirable it may be. For anyone to put himself in the position of another would be rarely feasible. That is why we appreciate Mo-tzŭ's idealism whereby the will of God is seen only in the experience of social outcasts. Comfortable men of prestige are almost always against the will of Supreme God who means equality. Confucius is right: We are not worried about poverty so much as inequality; chagrin due to inequality is more harmful than scarcity as such. Perhaps equalitarian zeal on the part of Confucius can be accounted for partly because he was a petty official's son and partly because of his appreciation of Heavenly harmony which is regarded as the basis for the political ideal of Jen. Compassionate use of power, prestige, possessions is the meaning of this ideal. Toward the end of his career, Confucius aimed all in vain to be reinstated as a high-ranking official of the Government. For six years he was like a homeless dog wandering from one place to another. One Autumnal day, late in the afternoon he would come to a mountain bridge where a pheasant would be startled by his coming, and fly up into the sky. But after a while the pheasant would see that Confucius had no intention of harming the bird. So the beautiful bird came down to the ground near where Confucius was philosophizing. Then he would think: " The pheasant knows when to fly and when to return to the ground: I too should know when to quit thinking about being reinstated as a statesman and when to switch to another task which is to begin to teach future statesmen in a school I should organize."   All this experience of his must have made his political philosophy more in line with the hope of the frustrated folk down at the bottom of the social ladder, when he came to teach this philosophy in the newly organized school to which he settled down.

*Book of Songs, Book of Changes, Discourse on Morals* are the classics teaching the political ideal of Jen. Merciful use of power on the part of the ruler is the message of Jen. Mencius, c. 390–305 B.C., adds the ideal of coorporate responsibility to it. Not only the ruler but also the citizen should be Jen-minded so as to realize just society modelled after Heaven. This would mean coorporate responsibility on the part of the ruler and citizens both. Mencius believed in the union of Heavenly Jen and Social Justice. His view of human nature was rooted in the sense of sympathy innate in every man. This spirit of sympathy must be nurtured by contemplation of Heavenly harmony. His pacifism is based on Heavenly harmony and his observation of every war which can be traced back to selfishness on the part of the ruler. There is no just war in history. A great citizen would be tempered by Heaven so as to have his inner life grow strong, noble, peaceful, heavenly, Jen-minded. Hardship accepted courageously strengthens the inner life of a good man. Problems are privileges. The Cosmic Class conducted by Heavenly Healer gives a great mission of peace-making, Jen-proclaiming, justice-doing.

The whole natural universe is a Marvlously Meaningful Milieu which serves as One Blissful Mental Inspiration. It is uplifting in some unusual sense. The support of this cosmic consolation is the hope of mankind. Mencius did his best in trying to convince rulers of China about this hope. He would teach citizens of Chinese nations about it too. His view of Nature must have been more spiritual than material, thus stressing the way it can enlighten, enliven, educate the human mind, which can be as flexible as the willow twig and as fluid as water. The mind at its best is teachable, docile, promising. Every citizen should aspire to become as Jen-minded as the best Emperor Wu in ancient China. That would not be impossible. " Wu is human: so are you." Filial piety, brotherly love, Heavenly decorum (Li) are what marked the best Emperor. International amity, world loyalty, devotion to Heaven would be the burden of the message of Mencius.

In this great crisis of history, standing in the midst of the atom age, we could learn from Mencius a special lesson of seeing in adversity a unique advantage in that what we would not try to do in a hopeful age we would be compelled to put into practice. A great crisis can be an occasion of realizing great genius. Trial brings out heroes.

Three great pleasures are enjoyed by the citizen as he is happy among dear ones in his own home; happy to sense heavenly approval of his good deed; happy to have chance to teach bright students in his school. He can raise cattle, silk worms, cultivate fields. There is happiness for the hard-working citizen. Temperance, diligence, rising early to enjoy his own work, being good to neighbors, old people, children would give him happiness too. There is happiness also in his having not only starting power but staying power so as to give a finishing touch to his life work. A good citizen would be just as important or even more important than the ruler himself. Without good citizens the ruler's state would not be good at all. A good ruler enjoyed three treasures: his land, people, statesmanship worthy of the name.

Mencius taught Jen, Justice, Heavenly Peace, so as to have them avoid acquisitiveness, utilitarianism, greed. When he was a child his mother would change her residence three times until he would come to love study in line with the custom of the environment of the new residence.

Mo-tzŭ would speak for an ex-criminal. The poet of the T'ang Dynasty speaks about an exile's point of view. Tu Fu 杜甫 probably is one of the most excellent poets of the 8th century. When the Emperor Genso 玄宗皇帝 and the Rare Beauty Yokihi 楊貴妃 were having a love affair, Young Tu Fu would struggle to be employed as a Government official. But his dream did not come true. Later he would get involved in a warfare. So he escaped with his family into safe areas in the Southwest. And he died aboard a ship, without fulfilling his hope of returning to his home city Choan 長安. He was 59 years old when he died.

Tu Fu's philosophy is marked by a few impressive ideas. First, life is so tragic as to cause good people to suffer unnecessarily. Second, the vicissitudes of history are all so remarkable. Third, it is so difficult to improve on social conditions, however hard good people pray, struggle, endeavor. Fourth, one consolation is the ways Nature comes to the rescue as if it were the extension of human friendship at its sweetest.

*Book of Songs* had been in China, teaching the necessity of emulating peace, order, harmony on the part of the beautiful universe. But men of prestige like the Emperor, statesmen, high-ranking officials would ignore this necessity. They misuse their power, causing the masses of people to suffer profoundly.

The Emperor would begin a war of aggression so as to extend his political influence into new territories, using men as victims for the realization of his greedy campaign. The Confucian ideal of Jen would be totally ignored. Mo-tzŭ's pacifism rooted in the will of Supreme God too would be entirely forgotten. As Plato in Athens points out, the newly gained prestige on the part of the ruler causes his nature to be transformed quickly into that of a wolf. This is applicable not only to Athens but to China where the people had been privileged to have moral teachings enshrined in *Book of Songs, Book of Changes, Annalects of Confucius, Discourse on Morals*. The Emperor's love of voluptuous women would be so strong as to ignore all the noble wisdom of Jen, Tao, Yin-Yang.

The concept of change has a special meaning for the poet like Tu Fu. His youthful aspiration of being a Government official, his dream of the realization of peace, order, justice in human society, his hope of returning to his native province would be all so dear and yet sadly illusory. Before any of these ideals begins to be fulfilled even to the slightest degree, time passes fast. Spring with its flowery glee in the Chinese continent; Summer with its splendid display of sunrises, clouds, greeneries; Autumn with its fruits, flavors, fragrances; Winter with its impressiveness white, frosty, frozen, mark the speedy recurrence of the four seasons. All the more, by contrast, this speediness is felt by the poet whose noble dreams never come true, unlike the dream of The Big Bird Taiho. At the age of forty six Tu Fu was already white-haired. Contracting tuberculosis he would be forbidden to enjoy even that cup of liquor which used to console him in those depressing moments of his. Thus he would be going upriver aboard a small ship, quietly, stealthily, fearfully, for any moment his enemies might come after him to kill him.

The idealistic poet in exile could not cope with the Emperor lustful. Acquisitive society of China would be on the side of the latter, while the former has appealed to millions of Chinese-speaking students in Asia, because Tu Fu has written about his method of helping, sheltering, saving poor victims of the sinful war. A vast mansion, in line with his dream, would be built so as to invite all those disinherited citizens of sad society. This is a ten-million-pillared mansion big enough to accommodate all the poor people, houseless, hopeless, horrified because injustices like exploitation, shame, insult, bereavement had impinged on those poor people such that this luxurious mansion would please them infinitely. And Tu Fu, single-handed, would build that mansion which symbolizes the Realm of Heaven here on earth. Sordid, acquisitive society could not be trusted. He would do all the work of building that palace. He alone would do all the entertaining necessary for making the exploited people well-fed, well-sheltered, well-contented.

No men of influence come to the rescue. But Tu Fu is consoled by sights, sounds, scents of Nature. China is a vast continent with mighty rivers, lakes, hills, forests, mountains, waterfalls, plains, cities, villages, rice fields, bamboo groves, birds, animals, flowers fantastically beautiful. The beauty, grandeur, sublimity of the Chinese Continent would be a striking contrast to the small-scale loveliness of the Japanese isles, peninsulas, colorful, vivid, picturesque. Even the moon would be large, continental, extra impressive in China.

> The River Moon is only a few feet away
> From me as I go upstream
> Aboard a small boat
>
> After midnight the river fish
> Fly above the shining surface
> of the dark water
>
> The Moon seems to have a message
> Specially consoling to me
> As I escape from enemies of mine

Nature cheers up the poet. The moon says, " Do not be dismayed, for I am with you always, so near you that you can almost reach me." Here is the continuation of the message of *Book of Songs* which all mankind should listen to in this atom age of ours. Not even the strongest enemy can take away Nature from the poet.


### B.   THE IMPOSSIBLE MADE POSSIBLE

Peace had not come in China. The dragon or Taiho able to fly from one end of the sky to the other means the realization of her dream. This is a foresight. Perhaps it is the voice of prephecy. Today in the age of jet planes and space flight we are attracted to the foresight of the Chinese antiquity. Superhuman ingenuity due to God is here dramatically depicted so as to urge mankind to deviate from the foolish ways of hateful activities into the the way of cosmic originality. In Heaven is at work True Teacher showing us the way to peace, truth, happiness.

God makes possible the humanly impossible. We must see in Him the only Trustworthy Lord worthy of our highest loyalty. He alone can do it. We should be still and be devoted to Him. Men alone in the wide world are self-willed. Dragons, birds, butterflies, cicadas all follow the harmonious way of Nature where peace prevails. Men should repent deeply, refraining from hating, fighting, complaining. No human boss is trustworthy. Power corrupts him. God immanent in Nature alone is dependable.

Zen, Jen, Tao, Yin-Yang, Christian love all stand for the will of God, Eternal Educator. As they come to think together, new ways to peace, truth, bliss, hope will be seen. Wall-removing among Love, Yin-Yang, Tao, Jen, Zen will be our first task of importance.

*C.* THE RULE OF JEN

> The East is poetic, aesthetic, peaceful
> The West is aggressive, acquisitive
> Arrogant, obsessed with power

> The East is interested in poise
> Blessedness, peace, courtesy
> Academic, athletic, appreciative

> Worldly success is stressed
> By the West too much
> At the expense of self-realization

> Westernized Japan with politicians
> Money-minded does injustice
> To the ideal of the East

> The idea of conquering Nature
> Does not bring happiness
> The Cosmic Class is our Teacher

> True Teacher is Eternal Educator
> While power-obsessed scholars
> Menace the university

> Money and power dominate
> The West, while virtue and
> Jen inspire the East

> The Tyrant is worse than tigers
> Jencracy (Rule of Jen) is better than democracy
> Compassion should enrich communism

Dharmanomy (Rule of Law), compassion, fascination
   Must supplement democracy
      Communism, fascism

Rule of Law means Buddha's view
   Of Cosmic Compassion (Law) construed
      As the basis for morals, religion, statesmanship

Buddha saw this Law through Zen
   Sustaining the human soul forever
      As the soul is enlightened into merciful Buddha

Zen practiced alone in the bosom
   Of Nature enables one to be enlarged
      Ennobled, enlightened into a boundlessly merciful soul

So Law (Dharma) is an Indian view
   Of Jen which is the Chinese version
      Of the same will of Heaven

Zen or Jen brings ecstasy or fascination
   Into the inner life of the enlightened soul
      Enjoying the highest bliss God-given

This bliss is due to the realization
   Of the only Truly Trustworthy Lord
      Worthy of man's consuming loyalty

Hence my reference to what I have
   Stressed already: Dharmanomy, compassion
      Fascination must enrich democracy, communism, fascism

The East has been more interested
   In ethics which culminates in politics
      Than the West interested in epistemology

The strong would be more in need
  Of ethics than the weak
    The former have made history bloody

The weak would not have the power
  Of making the centuries sick
    With cruelty, atrocity, war

Peace will never come until the strong
  Would come to have the spirit
    Of Jen, modelled after the will of Heaven

The Jen-minded ruler would take
  The whole responsibility for any wrong
    Causing the people to suffer

Right use of political power alone
  Would make the masses of people
    Well-fed, well-sheltered, well-contented

The unusually attractive blossoms
  Would symbolize the solicitation
    To make all see the need of Jen

Jen is so high but nothing
  Short of this is able to realize
    The dreams of the ages—peace


*D.* IF

    If Buddhism and Confucianism had come
      To Japan by way of Europe and America
        They would have taken on new meanings

If Christianity had come to Japan
  By way of India and China it would
    Have taken on a more subdued value

Hitler in Europe regarded his race
  As the Aryan master race while in India
    Caucasians had repented after the Aryan Invasion

Europe regarded Christ as Christ Conquering
  Whereas in Asia Christ would be
    Christ Consoling for the weak

A religion is a union of a *revelation claim*
  And a set of cultural traits
    Which vary from continent to continent

According to the Chinese classic, *Book of Changes*
  The Yin (feminine) virtues are superior
    To the Yang (masculine) traits

Today in our powerful age mankind would
  Need more feminine virtues in culture
    Religion, statesmanship and science

Sublimation of statesmanship, science
  Strength, prestige everywhere
    Into so many Yin virtues must be stressed

Thus and thus alone peace will come
  Justice will be realized in history
    And happiness will prevail here too

Hope will be here in you and me
  If through Zen we come to see
    The need of the above sublimation

Hope-kindler par excellence
Is Principle of Oneness in the cosmos
Whereby we are awakened to see Cosmic Support

*E.*   POETIC PLEAS

In this new age of ours
    *Book of Songs* has a message
        Specially apt, helpful, great

This Chinese classic urges us all
    To learn from Nature
        In all the four seasons

The rice plant would bow
    More and more lowly
        As it becomes truly ripe

Let us all bloom
    Like one big blossom
        Beautiful, benign and blessed

In this new age
    Where does Japan end
        Where does another nation begin

It is noble and sublime
    To see one's own self
        In the proud enemy

No teacher is
    Worthy to be called good
        Except Eternal Educator

The white jewel chipped
Can be polished
To regain its original form


Words carelessly uttered forth
Cannot be remedied
By any means


*F.*   BEYOND FIXED FORMS


*Book of Songs* mentions a lovely girl
Who knows how to smile enticingly
Her eyes are beautifully eloquent

She gives a finishing touch
To her make-up on the face
With a thin coating of white power

Here the uniquely Chinese concept
Of *Li*, courtesy or decorum, is
Hinted at as the above finishing touch

All the moral virtues are needed
By statesmanship whose finishing touch
Is akin to the white coating

Statesmen would need aesthetic values
So as to make foreign nations
Appreciate their statesmanship

Statesmen must study history, aesthetics
Philosophy, be athletic in a noble way
And stand for aesthetic values like courtesy

Academic, athletic, aesthetic
   Equivalents of war would be
      The message of Confucian Jen

*Book of Songs* urges statesmen and
   Citizens to go the second mile
      Going beyond stereotypes of society

## G.  SIDE RESULT

Happiness is brought as a side-result
   As one makes another happy
      Like a wife making her husband happy

The immediate aim of hers is the happiness
   Of his, which brings her happiness
      As a by-product or side result

This is why the feminine virtue
   Is regarded as a more blessed one
      Than the masculine trait of selfishness

*Book of Changes, I Ching* puts the Yin, feminine
   Before the Yang, masculine for the above reason
      The feminine subdual is nobler

The passive, indirect, self-sacrificing
   Quiet, altruistic virtue of a woman
      Would be more in line with Heavenly Harmony

Like a hidden dragon who is virtuous,
   One with Heaven, doing good secretly,
      A lady is the recipient of blessedness

Not only in the present generation
But in the ages to come, the Yin
Will receive more side blessings

First the frost falls, then thick ice is formed
Good will not be realized quickly
Only gradually, steadily, surely it comes

The hidden dragon will ascend
To Heaven in the end
As a side result of his good habit

*H.*  LIMITS

God's work is wonderful
Beyond the work of human mind
As to the art of limit operations

Modern math is just beginning
To see this art from a human point
Of view, way inferior to God's way

And yet many subtle meanings
Have been disclosed already
To mathematicians of our age

God unites all things different
From one another into one cosmos
Harmoniously unified and beautiful

Let us begin to learn from this course
In the tribute of *I Ching*
The way to the Yin-Yang union

As you marry in the near future
  Remember the charm of conjugation
    Symmetry you and your mate will form

Here in this matter let us see
  The secret to the harmonious union
    Of teacher and students learning together

The teacher can be more gracious
  Sweeter, more merciful toward them
    They can be more active, cooperative, appreciative


*I.* GOOD IN THE COSMOS

  The good is embedded in the cosmos
    Whereas moral evil is embedded
      In man's heart and in human society

  In *Book of Changes* ethic finds
    Its ultimate guidance in cosmology
      Or a cosmic set of Yin-Yang unions

  Cosmology is the Word of God
    Who realizes those Yin-Yang unions
      Exhaustively to explain ideal society to be

  Good means Yin-Yang harmony
    Bringing peace among all nations
      And some side results unexpected

  The good man is a dragon
    Who brings Yin-Yang harmony
      And is hidden in some noble way

His virtue is in line with Heaven
   And Earth where God brings
      Advance, growth, change

Buddha, Plato, Jesus, Spinoza, Whitehead
   All agree to the idea
      Of ethics embedded in cosmology

Dissimilarities among them are many
   But this agreement or similarity
      Would unite many human groupings

In this atom age of ours mankind
   Must see the ways to global unity
      One of them is seen here

Hence the real importance
   Of this way to global unity
      On which peaceful society must be built

Nature shows regularity, order, creativity
   Beauty, staying power, stick-to-itness
      Vast cooperation on the part of all things

Its vastness, sublimity, harmony
   Make us humble and see
      Humility, staying-power, creativity are needed
      by students

Brothers may fight inside the home
   They, however, will cooperate
      To cope with their enemy outside

This statement of *Book of Songs*
   Is applicable to the situation
      In which we find ourselves at ICU

The faculty, administration, students
　　May disagree but must be united
　　　　As outsiders ridicule us at ICU

They may say that "I" means isolated
　　"C" means crazy or cruel
　　　　"U" means useless

We hold that "I" means international
　　"C" ideals of Christ Creative, Consummating, Cosmic
　　　　"U" academic excellence

Generalize the above to see today
　　The nations must cooperate
　　　　As Nature sets the example of harmony

The atoms must laugh at mankind
　　If the nations cannot realize
　　　　Peace, order, mutual respect


*J.*　Sex Bliss Generalized

　　Sweet bliss in married life at its noblest
　　　　Should be extended into as many
　　　　　　Human relations as possible

　　This is the practical message we derive
　　　　From the Yin-Yang union realized
　　　　　　By God construed as Origin of Oneness

　　A good wife would sacrifice some of her own welfare
　　　　To make her husband or child blessed
　　　　　　This is the way to God's mercy

She becomes truly happy by making her family
  Happy, showing the value of sacrificial love
    Reminding us of God's boundless love

This book should come to embody some
  Of this sweetness, mercy, blessedness
    So as to enable all of us to be thankful

Sex love is to be seen as an occasion
  For guiding us into the realm of God
    Who is responsible for the harmony of Nature

This harmony shows a high religion
  Construed as the basis for statesmanship
    And international amity, peace, hope

Home at its sweetest comes first, then the state
  Made orderly, peaceful, just to usher in
    The global happiness, cooperation, bliss

All this is rooted in God's guidance
  Behind the Yin-Yang union
    Dramatically presented in *Book of Changes*

As science, aesthetics, math come to
  Fathom Nature more and more deeply
    The hints it gives grow richer and richer in meaning

Today physics shows conjugation symmetries
  Which unite elementary particles
    Into pairs of particles and antiparticles

This is a hint at the need of cooperation
  Akin to the sweet Yin-Yang love
    Between men and women on earth

Astronomy has disclosed 2 billion galaxies
   Evolving from nebulae into spirals
      From spirals into spheres

Physics and astronomy stimulate math
   To advance by leaps and bounds
      Hence group theory, matrix theory, advanced
         calculus

These new branches of modern math are
   Beautiful patterns of whole-seeing
      Generalization, interconnected oneness

The minutest analysis of math
   Has brought the vastest synthesis
      In line with Zen, *Book of Songs, Book of Changes*

The dream of the ages is coming true
   Beyond the expectations of the poets
      Prophets, dreamers of dreams

In *Book of Songs* no human teacher
   Is mentioned, implying that God alone
      Is able to teach

God uses attractive sights and sounds
   To teach cooperation, peace, kindness
      Harmony, mutual help, love

Education of students and teachers
   Ought to take place at the same time
      As God conducts His cosmic class

I as the conductor of this human class
   Should come here to study
      Under Cosmic Compassion, God

Not to punish but to perfect
Not to blame but to bless
Not so much to inform as to inspire is my task

Nature does not speak the way we do
But gives us hints which can be
Construed as ways to peace, hope, success

My book *Hints in Haiku*, is modelled
After the way of Nature in the sense
That the tiniest flower teaches infinitely

Haiku is the shortest form of poetry
But is rich in hints helpful
And inspiring as no preaching can be

Preaching often antagonizes; teaching fails
Hints in Haiku follow those
Of the world where God reigns

He who is not kind should not be
Called a philosopher whose personality
Is more important than his knowledge

Inspiration is more important
Than information, though it is true
New helpful information inspires

Kindness means sweet altruism plus
A new insight into the potential worth
Of the student who is ignorant of it

Humility, sweetness, ever new insights
Into potential worth in Nature
And human nature are needed

A mother's love for her own dear child
  Is here generalized into a more universal love
    For inherent worth in every one


If the student is frightened by the teacher
  This shows the teacher is not kind
    His kindness would be contagious


Many students dislike math
  Because their teacher is unkind
    Cross, haughty, unsympathetic


Math taught with kindness is
  Beautiful, convincing, consoling
    Math is the freest activity of the mind


The logic of math, which is interconnectedness
  Is essentially the same as that
    Of business, common sense, daily experience


*K.*  A REAL ROMANCE


    Kindness is what I would like
      To stand for as I conduct
        This course entitled Asian Thought


    In this class everything will be done
      In the spirit of thoughtful kindness
        Which will be heart-warming


    I consistently trust and love you beyond what
      You deserve so as to make you
        Have a rendezvous with your best self

The ideal self is waiting to be realized
  In you and I would like to point out
    That it is like a seed

As water, sunshine, care are given
  To it, it will begin to grow
    Into the realization of the ideal self

Becoming a good person
  Is the outcome of the romance of teaching
    Whose value is half hidden

The man is more important
  That the knowledge he has
    Inspiration more wonderful than information

*Book of Songs* 詩経 speaks about
  The man of wisdom 哲人 who learns
    From sights and sounds of Nature

The bamboos are growing harmoniously
  In the grove, the male and female birds
    On the bank of the river love each other

These sights of the Big, Beautiful Book
  Of Nature stand for the will
    Of God, Parent of Peace, Growth, Truth

The man of wisdom is quiet and careful
  About what he says for careless utterances
    Could not be remedied in any way

God is True Teacher kindly conducting
  The cosmic class after which this class
    Would like to be modelled

The charming blossoms
　　Called " totei " 唐棣 like graceful dancers
　　　　Beckon to us to be kind-hearted

Confucius would refer to them
　　As the Heavenly beckoning
　　　　To statesmen to bring global peace

Compassionate use of power on the part
　　Of men of prestige is symbolized
　　　　By lovely blossoms freely giving away aroma

*L.*　Men of Wisdom

In *Book of Songs* we find the concept *tetsu* 哲
　　Which means hidden hints which guide
　　　　Or hidden wisdom, that is, philosophy 哲学

The way to peace, bliss, hope is hidden
　　Behind sights, sounds, scents of Nature
　　　　Philosophy is to fathom this way

Not sight but insight is here stressed
　　For Nature hints at the insight
　　　　Into the way to peace, bliss, hope

This insight gained ennobles the man
　　Who is Jen-minded in the sense
　　　　Of beautifying his personality

The quality of the man is more important
　　Than the amount of knowledge he has
　　　　For he inspires and informs

Inspiration is superior to information
    The wise man exerts unconscious influences
        Upon all those with whom he comes into contact

Jen should make us transcend
    Name, gain, fame, self, praise, blame
        In order to be one with the universe

The superior man is selfless, the divine man
    Is meritless, the sacred man is nameless
        Just as Cosmic Coordination is selfless, nameless,
        meritless

The helpful hints given by Nature
    Are infinite, inexhaustible, immortal
        Urging mankind to grow indefinitely


*M.*   THE SON OF HEAVEN

*Book of Songs* poses problems which can be solved
    By having good rulers aspiring to emulate
        The harmony of Heaven where equality reigns

The problems the Chinese people had
    Were poverty, sex, liquor, heavy taxation, war
        Caused by unwise rulers

Unwise in that good men are not
    Used in strategic places while
        Bad cruel men who flatter the ruler are given good
        positions

War rages for a long time to cause
    Women to suffer unspeakably
        While their husbands are fighting abroad

Many years pass, in the meantime
  Their home provinces grow deserted
    Famine menaces the helpless

Rulers begin their wars because of lust
  For more power over other rulers' land
    Thus causing unjust, unnecessary wars

Beautiful young ladies become widows
  Spending sleepless nights, longing
    For their dreams of peace, bliss, hope

The wise ruler is a son of Heaven whose harmony
  Regularity, poise, sublimity, beauty
    Must be the symbol of his rule

So *Book of Songs* does not contain words
  By men of leisure but useful hints
    Aiming to change history into heaven

Unusual phenomena like mountain slides
  And river water growing boiling hot
    Are construed as God's warnings

Rulers are warned against tyranny
  So as to improve on their ways
    Of administering the governments

The rulers must be sons of Heaven
  Which is the symbol of fairness
    Justice, equality, peace, mercy

Strange happenings like typhoons ought to be
  Construed as special occasions
    For global repentance, rebirth, renewal

We are not rulers but aware
Of our shortcomings somewhere
In us or in our habits


Impatience, irritability, laziness
Unkindness, haughtiness, pride
All could be done away with


The cosmic Koan (Parable) which True Teacher uses
Is the song or sermon of poise
Which we are to live in human history


*N.* YIN STATESMEN

" President Nixon should have feminine hormones
Put into his system," said Miss Gloria Stimson
Pleading for calm behavior on his part


" Feminine virtues would bring calmness
In dealing with critical situations
While masculinity tends to bring excitement "


Miss Stimson is a newspaper reporter
Saying the above in a Florida conference
For newsreporters recently in 1971


This is in line with *Book of Songs*
Urging statesmen to emulate aesthetic values
Like Li 礼 to give a finishing touch to economic values


Something over and above necessities of life
Would be needed by the nations
Before peace, happiness, hope can come

*Book of Changes* would plead implicitly
   For the feminine-masculine cooperation
     On the part of East and West

Usually acquisitive, aggressive go-getters
   Become statesmen, while the ideals
     Of Li, Jen, Yin-Yang plead for feminine virtues

Patience, staying power, calmness, foresight
   Perspective would come through the Yin influence
     In the cosmos where Yin-Yang are harmonized

The Emperor and Empress of Japan leave Tokyo for Europe
   This morning after the typhoon 29 has cleared
     The sky for their plane to take off

They have a mission to fulfil this time
   In the sense of showing their Yin virtues
     To the nations in Europe and America

*O.*   27 SEPTEMBER 1971

     Peace does not come because the nations
       Do not go the second mile
         Rising above stereotypes

     Something unusual or extraordinary
       Must be done, otherwise
         Wars continue to menace history

     On the day the Emperor and Empress
       Flew to Europe by way of Alaska
         Tokyo was enjoying a fine day

Unusually numerous red dragon-flies
And crickets were heard and seen
Even in the center of Tokyo City

In Anchorage, Alaska an aurora
Appeared in the northern skies
Before their plane took off for Copenhagen

Auroras are seen only a few times
In Anchorage mostly in midwinter
But it appeared as the plane was about to take off

It changed color from orange to green
Pink and gold, making it unforgettable
For those who admired its splendor

" The Son of Heaven " 天子 is guided
By the signs of the skies, seas, storms
To fulfil the dreams of the ages


*P.*  THE EMPEROR TODAY

Time and time again the Emperor
Has saved Japan from going
The way of war

He was against the Pacific War
But Tojo's group began it
The Emperor urged us to stop fighting

Immature youngsters say today
The Emperor is a " War criminal "
Responsible for the Pacific War

Such an unreasonable blame
  Is what Zen would sublimate
    Into an occasion for enlightenment

The Emperor has been Zen-minded
  In dealing with General McArthur
    Radical students unfairly blaming him

He would be in the hottest fire
  Of hell so as to save those
    Who suffer from injustice

The Son of Heaven, the Emperor of Japan
  Stands for Heavenly beauty, harmony, peace
    Hence the sunny weather he ushers

17 October 1971 is a fine day since he is back
  In Tokyo, wherever he was in Europe
    The " weather man " was steeped in sunbeams

In Anchorage the rare appearance
  Of auroral flushes beautified
    The sky of the airfield as the plane took off

This is *Shih Ching* and *I Ching* in action
  In this century in Anchorage, Europe
    In this city of Tokyo

The Emperor's trip must have fulfilled
  Some meaningful mission
    Of which Heaven approves

He is a friend of Cosmic Buddha
  Succeeding in including all beings
    In the circle of boundless compassion

The Chinese ideal of Jen statesmanship
Has come to have the Zen expansion
To frame a union of Jen and Zen

The Emperor of Japan has studied Zen
Under Daisetsu Suzuki so as to include
All mankind in his circle of cosmic mercy

Harmony with Nature has thus come
To characterize his recent trip
To the nations in Europe

Zen sees no enemies anywhere for it embraces
All nations in the hands of mercy
Boundless, warm, inexhaustible

Zen prays for enlightenment of all mankind
Especially those who are victims of disturbances
Like anger, greed, hate, complaint

Appreciation of both Jen and Zen
Is the way of Japan at her best
Especially after Hiroshima


*Q.*   BEAUTY BRINGS SCIENCE

Beauty shows the way to statesmanship
At its best, noblest, most fruitful
Confucius would point this out

The Chinese classics like *Book of Songs*
*Book of Changes, Annalects*
All stress aesthetic values

Feminine virtues like grace, poise
  Calmness, subdual, patience, humor
    Charm, resilience are cases in point

Statesmen should not be brutes
  But noble souls beautified
    Through appreciation of Heavenly Harmony

Misusers of power should become
  Compassionate bestowers of gifts
    For the welfare of the minority groups

Beauty has been the way to science too
  Science and math have been guided
    By the pattern of symmetry

All apriori predictions in quantum theory
  Are rooted in the symmetries
    Of the natural environment

The beauty of Nature at its perceptual
  And quantum levels has guided
    Science to make new discoveries

Amazing side results disclosed
  Repeatedly and unexpectedly
    Show the divine source of science

The Yin, feminine, way is more successful
  Than the Yang, masculine, and is the spirit
    Of the Japanese art of self-defence, Judo

The more patient, skillful, feminine
  Will be able to cope with the Yang
    More forceful, active, positive

Mr. Mifune was a small man
Who could beat any Judo men
In those days when I studied Judo

He was like a swallow
Swift, agile, moving like the wind
Defending himself under any circumstances

The sage described as " tetsujin " 哲人
In *Book of Songs* would be
The " dragon " in *Book of Changes*

The dragon flies from the horizon
To the zenith, bespeaking the prophet
Who sees things in perspective

Rising above provincialism in space
And time, the dragon-philosopher
Sees the total truth

Buddha uses the same word, naga 竜 (dragon)
Which means without sinfulness (na+āga)
In the most ancient sutra, *Suttanipāta*


R.   GOD, ORIGIN OF ONENESS

The Yin-Yang union of *I Ching*
Has marked one of the most impressive unions
Of modern seience in this age of ours

Since 1966 the Japanese Nobel Prize physicist
Dr. Yukawa has worked on the union
Of matter and time fruitfully

The atom (Greek) construed as " elementary particle "
  And the shortest span of time, Kṣaṇa (Indian)
    Have been united into " elementary domain "

This new union of the Greek and Indian views
  Is in line with *I Ching*, for time is Yin (feminine)
    And matter is Yang (masculine)

This is framed in accordance with Einstein
  Whose general relativity theory means
    The interrelated oneness of matter, mind, time, space

In another words, all things in the universe
  Are interwoven with one another
    As Zen shows it by a reed-stack

Here the English mathematician-philosopher
  A. N. Whitehead is reminded of, for he sees
    God, Origin of Oneness, who makes all things grow
      together

This God is Source of Science, Parent of Philosophy
  Mother of Mathematics, who makes us see
    These traditions, Indian, Chinese, Greek cohere

Thus the New Testament view of the coherence
  Of all things or traditions in God, Colossians 1: 17
    Is being verified by Einstein, Whitehead, Yukawa

The most general version of this coherence
  Is nothing but the Zen insight into oneness
    Of all events, essences, entities

In this atom age we members of mankind
  Must be united so as to restore peace
    In all the world which must not be divided

The present moment (καιρὸς) here and now is
>Most crucially important in that we must repent
>>And pray for the coming of global peace

This reminds us of the teaching of Jesus
>Enshrined in Mark 1: 15 to the effect
>>That the right time (ὁ καιρὸς) has come

Indeed this is the right time for global repentance
>For we still do not believe in humility, love
>>Universal brotherhood, peace, cooperation

Our present time is not only the Indian kṣaṇa
>But the divine moment καιρὸς when we
>>Must rededicate ourselves to God

When we say God, we mean not only the Biblical God
>But also the God of *I Ching*, who unites
>>Harmoniously all Yin-Yang, East and West, Ethics and Science

All disciplines of civilization, statesmanship
>International relations, aesthetics, religion
>>Must become one in their devotion to God

God is Origin of Oneness, who alone can
>Bring peace, global unity, humility
>>Doing away with hate, division, war

## *S.* GROUP-MINDED

See various views in perspective
>Enjoy the group of them (dragons, *I Ching*)
>>Framing a more meaningful whole

This is the claim of the East
    Coinciding with the claim
        Of modern math and physics

The Eastern (Upanishadic) insight into Nature saw
    Atman, ἀτμός, the minutest unit
        Of Nature construed spiritually

It means the religious aspiration
    Of the soul to emulate goodness
        Akin to that of the Highest

The Western insight into Nature saw
    Atom, ἄτομος, the uncut atom
        Construed as the material stuff, Nature's minutest unit

The Western idea of man's conquest
    Of Nature is rooted in the view
        Of material atoms which constitute Nature

The Chinese idea of our learning
    From Nature is in line with the Atman view
        Aspiring to be one with God in Nature

Today the advance of physics is such as to see
    In atoms energetic activities akin to those
        Of the mind, thus uniting Greece and India

The three universes, material, mathematical, mental are
    Marked by conjugation symmetries which come
        Under universal interdependence Zen-oriented

These marks are all mathematical groups
    Thus leading Sir James Jeans
        To see God's Great Thought in the cosmos

God is a Pure Mathematician who keeps
   The structure of the universe
      Beautifully mathematical always

This is in line with *I Ching*, saying that math
   Mastered will disclose the meaning of being
      In the future years

*T.*   BOOK OF CHANGES *(I CHING):* IN THE LIGHT OF TODAY

The most profound explanation
   Of the cosmos mankind has
      Ever inherited from a Chinese antiquity

Only the resourceful mind
   Of this century of ours would be
      Able to understand, use, appreciate it

*Book of Songs* begins with affection
   Uniting a male and a female birds
      Symbolizing the love of God 能和睦者

Peace and harmony God wills
   Will bring peace in human society
      This theme is elaborated on in *I Ching*

All things in the whole universe
   Are made of Yin-Yang unions
      Through God's work of unification

The symbol "- -" is feminine
   " — " is masculine, which are
      Akin to Greek atoms or Indian Atmans

This is a queer idea but seems
  To make sense as civilization advances
    Disclosing many Yin-Yang unions


In the universe of math —, +mark
  Negative and positive numbers
    The imaginary numbers i, $i^2$, $i^3$, $i^4$ . . .


Enrich the situation, $i^2 = -1$, thus changing
  All positive numbers a into $-ai^2 = -a \times (-1) = a$
    $z = re^{i\theta}$, $\bar{z} = re^{-i\theta}$, $\bar{z} \cdot z = re^{i\theta} \cdot re^{-i\theta} = r^2$


The Yin-Yang union is conjugation
  Which means cooperation through bearing
    The yoke on the part of negative-positive beings


According to a Chinese Nobel Prize
  Winning physicist, Dr. C. N. Yang
    30 elementary particles are 15 conjugation symmetries


For instance the electron (e⁻) and
  The positron (e⁺) form a conjugation
    Symmetry, thus illustrating the Yin-Yang myth


Modern logic uses four equations
$$(\forall_x)(\phi_x \supset \psi_x) = \sim(\exists_x)(\phi_x \sim \psi_x) \qquad [+ + = - -]$$
$$\sim(\forall_x)(\phi_x \supset \psi_x) = (\exists_x)(\phi_x \sim \psi_x) \qquad [- + = + -]$$
$$(\forall_x)(\phi_x \sim \psi_x) = \sim(\exists_x)(\phi_x \supset \psi_x) \qquad [+ - = - +]$$
$$\sim(\forall_x)(\phi_x \sim \psi_x) = (\exists_x)(\phi_x \supset \psi_x) \qquad [- - = + +]$$
  Showing general or existential statements
    As A, E, I, O ($\sim$ means negation; $\supset$ coordination;
      $\forall_x$ all members of the class x; $\exists_x$ some members
      of the class)

This is the beginning of a more coherent
    Account of the three universes united
        By modifications of the Yin-Yang tale

"All things are made of Yin-Yang unions"
    Stated in *Book of Changes* will
        Someday come to be verified more convincingly

This is the prophecy of *I Ching* in this age
    Of ours, as the history of mankind
        Stands at a critical juncture

Between 1890 and 1962 eleven new
    Elementary particles were predicted
        Or foreseen before verified

Nagaoka (proton), Yukawa ($\pi$ meson)
    Sakata—Tanikawa—Inoue ($\mu$ meson)
        Sakata—Tanikawa—Inoue ($\mu$ neutrino)

Have been successful foreseers of those
    Making me think of *Book of Changes;*
        " Master math and foresee the future "

Japan does not have the laboratories
    Which Western nations like America
        Have but has been good in math

For this refer to Dr. Yukawa's book
    *Elementary Particles*, Second Edition
        Page 82, Iwanami, 1969, Tokyo

Yukawa's speculation about elementary domains
    Is another creatively audacious attempt
        Giving a finishing touch to his work

He may win a second Nobel Prize
   For this new study which may turn
      Out to be greater than his first success (1935)


Thus Japanese and Chinese scientists
   Are making creative contributions
      To the world of science


The Indian concept of the shortest span of time,
   And the smallest unit of matter are united
      Into his elementary domains


If time is feminine and matter is masculine
   This union is another form of Yin-Yang
      Conjugation symmetry


As Christ says, the tradition
   Is not abolished but achieved
      So as to show us the way to a better future


*U.*   BEAUTY IN YIN-YANG


Beauty means some forms
   Of symmetry or harmony of proportions
      Like faces, flowers, patterns of math


Simple, straightforward symmetry is
   Not so beautiful as conjugation symmetry
      Which is the union of Yin-Yang and symmetry


Mechanical, boring, impersonal is
   Symmetry pure and simple
      Conjugation is romantic, creative, dynamic

    Odd numbers are masculine
        Even numbers are feminine
            The integers are conjugation symmetries


    Organic worlds are often five-angled (star fish)
        Inorganic worlds often six-angled (snow flakes)
            Odd numbers are masculine; even feminine


    Cosine functions are even functions [cos $(-\theta)=\cos \theta$]
        Sine functions odd functions [sin $(-\theta)=-\sin \theta$]
            $(d/dx) \sin x = \cos x, (d/dx) \cos x$
                $=-\sin x, (d/dx)(-\sin x)$
                $=-\cos x, (d/dx)(-\cos x) = \sin x$


    Continuous differentiation of the sine function
        Brings a sequence of conjugation symmetries
            Plus a sequence of plus and minus signs


    Thus the more general meaning of beauty
        Is unity (d/dx) amidst diversities (m, f, $+$, $+$; f, m,
        $+$, $-$; m, f, $-$, $-$; f, m, $-$, $+$)
            Coherence among various data


    God, Origin of Oneness, Harmony
        Of Harmonies, Cosmic Coherence
            Is seen in beauty



*V.*  GOD, LIMIT LUSTRE


    Two different traits, female and male
        Are harmonized as limit into one union
            Beautiful, blessed, benign, in line with *I Ching*

This is the work of God, Principle
    Of Concretion as A. N. Whitehead calls
        God makes all things grow harmoniously as limit

Mind and matter are different
    But harmonized as limit into one universe
        Of space and time, mathematically construed

The most wonderful technique whereby mind
    Has come to understand the universe
        Is calculus which is a set of *limit* operations

Students and teacher, employees and employer
    One race and another race, East and West
        Old and New, Love and Zen, should be united

Limit operations of not only quantitative
    But also qualitative kinds will be possible
        Through God's work of harmonization

If mankind is to survive the crisis
    Of this nuclear age we all must
        Come to look up to God, Limit Luminous

God alone can teach mankind the secret
    To the art of limit operations
        Which can unite conflicting entities

Zen is beginnig to be verified in this age of ours
    When modern math, new physics, symbolic logic
        Are whole-seeing to show the oneness of the universe

Zen has long pointed out the hidden oneness
    Of all events in all ages like the reed-stack
        Binding all the separate reeds to form a unity

This time-honored insight would be laughed at
  By those who believe in the testimony of sight
    Showing separations, tensions, contradictions


In our age nuclear destruction could ruin the whole
  Civilization of ours if the tensions should aggravate
    Into a real nuclear warfare anywhere


The Cosmic Compassion, True Teacher, Origin of Organic
Oneness
  Adventurous Awakener shows His grace by making
    Math, physics, logic see the true unity of the cosmos


This unity is adorned with the conjugation patterns
$e^{-i\theta}, e^{i\theta}; e^{-}_{=}, e^{+}; \sim(\exists x)(\phi_x \sim \psi_x) = (\forall x)(\phi_x \supset \psi_x)\ [--=++]$
  In the mathematical, physical, logical universes
    Framing one Group three-dimensional


In line with *Book of Songs* 詩経 mankind must
  Be urged to learn these lessons of conjugation
    So as to frame a unified cosmos in history


Christ's prayer for the realization of the unified cosmos
  In human society is modelled after the Heavenly Realm
    Where God, Heavenly Father, realizes peace


In Christ all Agamas (traditions) cohere, Colossians I: 17
  In that Yin-Yang, Zen, Love (Christ), math, quanta, logic
    Come dovetailing into one another in our age


Global peace will come if more people come
  To see this cosmic coordination realized
    Through Eternal Educator, Adventurous Awakener,
    Limit Lustre

The missionary movement in China has failed
To do justice to the valid insights of Jen, Tao, Zen
While upholding Christ Conquering

Uneducated Christians ignorant of math, physics, logic
Zen, Jen, Tao, Yin-Yang tried to declare
The victory of Christ Conquering isolated

Christ isolated from insights of the East, math
Quanta, logic set-theoretical means nothing
Except bluffing on the part of the ignorant

Christ Coordinating has come to reveal God
Construed as Association Awakener
Through whom all traditions (Agamas) come together

Christ Consummating, Christ Consoling, Christ Coherent
Are here spotlighted through His appreciation
Of Samaritan insights into math, quanta, Zen

" The lilies of the field are beautiful without toiling "
So saying Jesus would inculcate the value
Of beautiful goodness which does not strain itself

Spontaneous, aesthetic, feminine values are
Appreciated by Christ, Confucius, Buddha
Zen, Jen, Tao, Yin-Yang, Yamato (peace)

Most people are quarrelsome, irritable
Argumentative, haughty, thus missing
The delightful experience of Zen ecstasy

God is Anger Annihilator, Shame Sublimator, Changing
Despair into delight even in the saddest situation
Where sorrow is sublimated into sacredness

*W.* RENDEZVOUS WITH THE IDEAL SELF

There is hope in your having a rendezvous
  With the ideal self till the latter becomes
    Your real self enlightened as a Buddha

God must be Explanation for Everything
  So as to account for all things in the universe
    Functioning as Accounter for All

Marvelous Mathematician, Energizer of Elementary
  Particles, Mother of Minds, Unifier
    Of the Universe, Source of Space-Time

Source of Symmetry, Cause of Conjugation
  Yielder of Yin-Yang, Source of Science
    Cause of Civililization is God

Origin of Oneness, Permanent Peace
  Bliss Bestower, Imparter of Insight
    Insurer of Immortality, Hope Hereafter


*X.* ANGER ANNIHILATOR

Anger is not a sign of moral strength
  But a confession of one's inner weakness
    Since he is unable to control himself

In the West God is angry whereas in the East
  God is Boundless Mercy whose circle of concern
    Would include all recalcitrant forces

Anger distorts our evaluation putting us all
  In disadvantageous positions, while forgiveness
    Enables us to fulfil our God-given missions

The stain of anger may be washed away
 In the sea of boundless mercy through which
  We come to pray for the repentance of the evil

Stay away from anger-provoking situations
 As much as possible whereas prayer or Zen
  In a quiet place will cure the mental wounds

Anger goes with acquisitiveness, arrogance
 Aggression which are all harmful to the health
  Of men and nations, especially in our age

A Japanese Zen master, just before he died, compared his
long career
 To one consistent success in mastering anger, sublimating
  It into broad mercy, work of tension-easing, hope-
   kindling

This can be done here and now as we conduct
 This course in Asian Thought, which gives us
  The blessed way to all-forgiving compassion

Oneness of life everywhere means the one togetherness
 Of the ocean of organic unity rooted in God
  Construed as *Anger Annihilator Par Excellence*

When Nature with its stars, clouds, hills, oceans
 Flowers, leaves, breezes are with me
  Who can be against me in the long run?

He who has completed the Zen experience
 Of being enlightened into Tathāgata 如来
  Which means Total Truth is Buddha

The mind at its best is space-transcending
 And time-transcending, seeing
  Interconnectedness of old and new views

This philosophical mind is moral
  Receiving the good consequences
    Of his forefather's goodness

He will enjoy good side results
  Unexpectedly and beyond what he deserves
    In line with the prophecy of *I Ching*

The House of accumulated good will enjoy necessarily
  Unexpected side results which are
    More blessed than the highest expectations

Here the Source of Side Splendor
  That is God, Limit Lustre, is
    Spotlighted to cheer up all human beings

Necessity is missed by Western thinkers
  Like David Hume, 1711–1776, who are guided by
  perception
    But the perspective of history gives necessity


Y.  NON-ACTION

In December 1971 India is fighting Pakistan. This is regrettable
for India is the birthplace of Buddha whose boundless compassion is supposed to include all mankind. India should not do
what is against Buddha's teaching of mercy, peace, seeing no
enemy anywhere.

Lao-tzŭ has taught non-action construed as the way of the
universe. Mo-tzŭ has taught universal peace, love, wisdom seen
in the despised people. All these Eastern principles are being
violated by the Eastern nations, India and Pakistan.

Japan after Hiroshima has come to see the necessity of peace.
This essay is a most sincere prayer for global peace. It is a
heartfelt appeal to every person in the world so as to realize

global peace as soon as possible. As Mencius says, " There is no just war in history." Christ is right, "All who take the sword will perish by the sword." India must see Rāhula in Pakistan. India is fighting herself by fighting Pakistan. All the nations of the world are one precious togetherness rooted in God. Communist China, Infuriated India, Anxious America are tragedies of today. Withdrawing and winning go together. Wisdom, wit, winsomeness are one.

## Z.   My Last Hope

The reader of this book is asked to be ingenious. His original, creative, adventurous ingenuity is our last hope. One-thousand-handed Buddha is a symbol of boundless ingenuity for helpfulness. Modern math has advanced in part because it has been unusually rich in techniques and arguments. Problems of racial inequality are ominous. The ideal of equality or compassion must be applied to these problems which aggravate almost all the difficult problems of the civilization of this age of ours. The primitive myth of the supremacy of the White race must be done away with as soon as possible. The Black, Yellow, White races will have to come to see that the principle of racial, sexual, class equality alone would solve all these problems. Higher education, intermarriage, religion, ethics like Zen, Jen, Tao, Love all are unanimous in stressing the global need of breaking down the above myth, not only theoretically but also practically. Children of mixed blood are not only goodlooking but also more intelligent than those children born of parents who are close to each other racially, ethnically, culturally.

Our appreciation of differences is thus verified from the point of view of our producing better children through intermarriage. This is opposed to Hilter's claim that the pure Caucasian race is the master race of history. Likewise we would deplore a a primitive religion which is absolutized that it would not be enriched by new findings of science, math, modern civilization.

Such a religion has caused wars so often in history. Once again we admire someone who was a Jew but saw goodness in a Samaritan who was a person of mixed blood.

The reader of this essay is urged to hit upon new meaningful insights whereby history will be brightened. " Panic of error is the death of progress," as A. N. Whitehead points out in his book, *Modes of Thought*. You are asked to be original, adventurous, path-finding. Dream the dreams of the ideal self, the ideal society, the ideal world. Your beautiful dreams will come true through the grace of God, the Cosmic Source of Side Splendor. Unexpectedly wouderful side results will thus be brought about.

The last part of our last hope is this: any adverse criticism of this book and its content is appreciated in line with the principle of appreciation of differences, the ampersand, heterodoxy-honoring. The resourcefulness of the universe is infinite, inexhaustible, inscrutable. God is Infinite Inexhaustibility, Ultimate Unexpectedness, Holy Heterodoxy. More and more convincing ways to the Holiest Hope, Highest Heterodoxy, Supreme Samaritan will be paved by people of originality. Total Truth must be greater, vaster, richer than all the findings of religion, science, aesthetics.

Deep insights of West and East
   Will mutually enrich
      One another


Haiku would describe life
   As one writer sees it
      In its entirety


Zen, Love, Jen pray together
   To pave the way
      To the Holiest Hope

The best is yet to be
  As mankind looks up
    To Him, the True Teacher

Curtain-lifting among Love
  Zen, Jen, Tao, Math
    Would be needed today

## LETTERS BY LOVED ONES

19 January 1970
3082-B Tachikawa Air Base
Tachikawa, Tokyo

Doctor Iino,

Please accept this poem which I wrote as a very small token of appreciation for your kindness and friendship. Your compassion and good will was very inspiring to me. I feel that you have made me go one step further into the person I dream to be. Thank you.

To Doctor Iino

There is about you sincerity overflowing
    A serene disposition of infinite worth
        That enshrouds those fortuate who know you

You possess a stemming kindness and a sparkling joy
    Which I've never known to exist in any one before
        And the calmness you command can ease the hottest soul

From here, my heart, I speak these words
    And pray they bear some meaning
        Be it soft, or sweet, or kind, or not

But let me swear to you how your presence
    Made me glad, and how your words of wisdom
        Made me so aware and aspiring

I'd so often wondered, Why?
    Wherefore do these " things " reign?

But answers never seemed to come and I remained
untold

You've made such
   Good things happen
     And I've gratitude galore!

And I just wish
   There was a way
     I could tell you evermore

That your life on earth is grand; majestic, great, warm
   And I'll remember—when I'm blue: I'll think of your
   prayer for me,
     And all the trust you gave to me, much beyond what I
     deserved

                        Thankfully yours,
                        *Midori Trent*

Dear Dr. Iino,

First, please let me express my appreciation to you for being
so understanding and kind to me. I was quite concerned about
my school work, but you were kind enough to take away
reason for my concern. I thank you very, very much.

Dr. Iino, you have succeeded in enlightening me, at least in
a sense. By your example, I have learned to see the good side
of everyone. I believe that I now place the benefit and comfort
of others above those of myself. I now look at the world in
general more optimistically.

You spoke in class on several occasions about an ideal person.
If I had to choose such a person that I have actually known, I
would undoubtedly choose you or someone like you. I'm not
saying this to put myself in your favor; it's the truth. You really

care about people. You are selfless and charitable.

Anyhow, Dr. Iino, it was indeed a privilege to be a member of your class. I hope to take your class next term.

Very truly yours,
*Randy Cook*

*Gratitude*

Heaven shows appreciation
The humble star shines bright
A grateful star will never forget
The reason for its light

12 May 1968

Dr. Iino,

It is sad, after three semesters of studying the conjugacy of ideals, that you must leave us here at Tachikawa, Dr. Iino, and I will perhaps never again have the privilege of studying with you. Your knowledge of so many cultures has given me many new insights with which I hope I can do my part to bring peace to our troubled world.

You have often spoken of beauty, and shown an appreciation of many things. I don't know if anyone has ever given you a psychedelic picture before but, I often draw them on occasions so I would like you to have this one. I hope you will find as much beauty in it as you have in so many things. Because you have shown this attitude toward me, I have many times gone ahead with many things which ordinarily I would have given up as complete failures.

Dr. Iino, you have aided me in so many ways, and I feel I must now thank you in the best way I know how. It is the purpose of the following poem to express my sincerest gratitude and appreciation for you during the short time we have studied together. The poem is entitled *Gratitude*, and I have written it with the deepest sincerity. I hope you will like it and, whenever you should read it, I hope you will think of me, your classmate, as I shall never forget you. Thank you, again, for everything.

Sincerely,

*John Reiner*

*Dedication*

To Dr. Iino
  I dedicate
    This book of poems

So wise a man
  So kind is he
    To all of us

Inspiring
  Imaginative
    Intuitive

A friend to me
  To all of you
    Now and forever

*Michael Malina*

*Amida* (Cosmic Buddha)

" I agree with you, Joe,
  You are so right ",
    The Christian professor said.

" Like you I have heard
  Those bigots who shout
    Noisily in Christ's name.

" I must confess
  For enlightenment
    I've studied Zen, Buddhism, too.

" The monks do find
  Love, Beauty, Peace of Mind,
    In quiet concentration ".

Joe smiled, relieved,
  For at last he'd found
    Someone who really understood.

What turmoil there is
  In the mind of a man
    In searching for the Truth.

By taking one step back
  The professor helped
    Joe to walk forward two.

It was then
  To Joe's open, eager mind
    The professor made his point.

" It's not religions
   That are bad
      But the sordid and bigoted men ".

Please, God, give us students
   More men who inspire
      Like Dr. Iino

We can do without
   Those who feed us facts
      We forget once the term's past.

*Mary E. O'Connor*

Vancouver, British Columbia
11 July 1969

Dear Dr. Iino,

So long ago I was one of your students at ICU—we together as a class, as two people after class and as small groups in your office would sit and talk about the world and life. It was so long ago that we talked with each other but still over the years I have thought about you and about what I learned in my year at ICU. Out of all my classes none have helped me so much as those three classes of yours. For those were times I was able to think, to write, to learn once more to create, I wrote Haiku before your class but from your class I went away with a greater understanding of Haiku as well as Japanese ethics and a beginning of understanding of myself and my relation to the world.

The reason I write at this time is that when I was with you at ICU you were planning to publish a book—so every once in a while when I was at a library I have looked up your name to see if your book has come out. Well, a few weeks ago I looked up your name and found that your book was listed—*Hints in Haiku*, by Philosophical Library. So I took the book out and have read it—which was like once more being in your class in Mitaka, Tokyo.

You have so many students over the years that I do not believe you would remember me, but if you do my name is Gordon.

The purpose of this letter has only been to let you know that one of your students who shared his first year of college did so in your class. I had lived in Japan for 15 years but learned more about Japan during my one year at ICU than all my other years. Also I want you to know that so much of making that one year at ICU so important in my growth was being able to share it in your class. The year after we spent together we both went to the U.S.A. Since that time I have been to Europe and am now living in Canada, as I have refused to serve in the American Army.

Well, to end let me just thank you for all you have done and I want you once more to know your book has been happily read by a former student of Peace.

*Shantik Gordon*

20 August 1965

Dr. Iino,

May I tell you of the great honor it has been to know even this small part of you as my professor. Your beauty overwhelms me. I shall always remember you and the great love that is so much a part of you—a love that you bring to all.

*Linda B. Warren*

Boston University

Wellman, Iowa
July 5 1965


Appreciation for
The Visit of a Professor, Poet, Prophet
Under whom I studied at ICU, Tokyo in 1963


Parting
      Your coming—a ride while
        The sky flashed with light
          Tonight, no words through
          The cool dark evening


Independence Day—
      Not fire works, but perceptive thoughts
        Bring spontaneous exclamation


(Understanding)
      Return from Japan
        How to explain the change?
        No, Japan comes to us


The willow tree can enjoy
      Even the wind
        Iino on the farm


This week Iino
      Stayed at our Iowa farm
        Moon and sweet clover


An appreciative church
      Plans a gift of gratitude
        But moves slowly

The poet expresses appreciation<br>
  To these matter-of-fact folk<br>
    Living new life

Quietly sitting on the bench<br>
  His words take us<br>
    Even beyond the evening horizon

Interesting and ever rewarding<br>
  The realization of Peace<br>
    As the beautiful will of God<br>
      (thank you for this thought)

Two hundred million galaxies<br>
  A visit we can not fully<br>
    Comprehend and appreciate

An unexpected reunion<br>
  The unwanted parting is<br>
    A little less poignant

Ashamed of not noticing many needs<br>
  We pray that our most appreciated guest<br>
    Will not remember us unkindly

Our prayers will surely follow<br>
  This unassuming<br>
    Bringer of blessings

*Carol Yoder*